JAPANESE-AMERICAN RELATIONS IN THE 1970's

Edited by Professor Gerald L. Curtis

THE AMERICAN ASSEMBLY

Japanese-American Relations in the 1970s

WASHINGTON, D. C.

COLUMBIA BOOKS, INC., PUBLISHERS

1 9 7 0

Library of Congress Catalog Card No.: 78-106895
SBN-910416-11-7

Printed in the United States of America for the Publishers
by
Publication Press, Inc.
Baltimore, Maryland

Table of Contents

Gerald L. Curtis, Editor

INTRODUCTION   vi

1. *Fuji Kamiya*
TOWARD A NEW ERA IN JAPANESE-
AMERICAN RELATIONS   1

2. *Marius B. Jansen*
THE UNITED STATES AND JAPAN
IN THE 1970s   20

3. *James William Morley*
GROWTH FOR WHAT? THE ISSUE
OF THE 'SEVENTIES   48

4. *Saburo Okita*
JAPANESE ECONOMIC COOPERATION IN
ASIA IN THE 1970s   94

5. *George McT. Kahin*
THE FUTURE OF UNITED STATES POLICY
IN SOUTHEAST ASIA   114

6. *Mineo Nakajima*
PEACE IN ASIA IN THE 1970s: COEXISTENCE
AND COMPETITION WITH THE "SHADOW
OF CHINA"   140

7. *Gerald L. Curtis*
AMERICAN POLICY TOWARD JAPAN IN THE
SEVENTIES: THE NEED FOR
DISENGAGEMENT   157

FINAL REPORT OF THE SECOND JAPANESE-
AMERICAN ASSEMBLY   181

Preface

The Second Japanese-American Assembly, sponsored by the Japan Council for International Understanding and The American Assembly, met in Shimoda, Japan, September 4-7, 1969. As in the first Assembly, also held in Shimoda, in 1967, the participants (70 in all) included scholars, government officials, businessmen and communication specialists from both nations.

For three days in small groups they discussed the outlook for the bi-national relationship in the 1970s in the light of present political, economic and social postures in each nation as well as in other countries of Asia.

The participants also heard formal addresses by Shojiro Kawashima, vice chairman of Japan's Liberal Democratic Party and Kogoro Uemura, president of the Federation of Economic Organizations; and by United States Senator Charles Percy of Illinois and Edwin O. Reischauer, former United States Ambassador to Japan.

In plenary session on the final day the participants reviewed a Final Report, which had been drafted by co-editors Gerald Curtis and Fuji Kamiya and by the discussion leaders and rapporteurs: Jun Eto, Hans Baerwald, Herbert Passin, Masataka Kohsaka, Marius Jansen, and Michio Rohyama. The Report appears in this volume beginning on page 181.

The chapters which follow, originally prepared as background reading for participants in the second Shimoda Assembly, are presented here for the general reader as edited by Professor Curtis. Together with *The United States and Japan* (ed. Passin, Prentice-Hall, Inc., 1966) they provide a comprehensive review of Japanese-American relations since World War II.

The views contained herein are the authors' own and not of the Japan Council for International Understanding or of The American Assembly, a non-partisan educational organization which takes no stand on issues it presents for public discussion. Nor is The Ford Foundation, which generously underwrote the costs of the Shimoda Assembly on the American side—gratefully acknowledged herewith—to be associated with the opinions on these pages.

Clifford C. Nelson
President
The American Assembly

Introduction

One of the authors writing in an earlier American Assembly volume on Japanese-American relations remarked that "For the last twenty years United States-Japanese relations have remained the central focus of [Japan's] international relations, and our foreign policy debates have been formulated almost entirely in terms of the pros and cons of the American alliance."[1]

The situation in the United States is in striking contrast to this. Japan receives little attention in the mass media and in discussions of American foreign policy until there is a boycott in the Diet or mass demonstrations in the streets against the Security Treaty. This is largely unavoidable because of the great number of events and places competing for the attention of those interested in foreign affairs. But there is a danger that when a crisis does occur, debate may be marked by a lack of information on the issues involved and by a tendency to be solely concerned with the most immediate crisis issue and indifferent to more fundamental questions.

As the "Security Treaty struggle" increases, Japan will almost surely receive greater attention in the United States than at any time since 1960 when the present Security Treaty was ratified. It is important that people interested in Japanese-American relations see this issue within its broader context. The crucial issue is not Japanese-American

[1] Kinhide Mushakoji, "The View From Japan," in Herbert Passin, ed., *The United States and Japan* (New Jersey, 1966), p. 129.

relations in 1970 but in the 1970's. It is to an analysis of this decade in the relationship that the seven authors of the papers in this volume address themselves.

Each author brings his own particular skills and concerns to an analysis of the coming years in the relationship. Fuji Kamiya, the co-editor of these papers as originally prepared for the second Japanese-American Assembly, addresses himself to a discussion of the ongoing changes in the international political system and the challenges and opportunities they present for Japan and the United States. Marius Jansen looks at Japanese-American relations in historical perspective and at the implications for foreign policy of trends present in contemporary Japanese society. James Morley provides a projection of Japanese public policy in the coming years by analyzing the likely allocation of Japan's economic resources. Saburo Okita brings his skills as an economist and specialist on Southeast Asia to an analysis of Japanese economic involvement in Asia. George Kahin's analysis of American policy in Southeast Asia provides an important perspective for discussion of Japanese-American relations as does Mineo Nakajima's article on China's international relations. In the concluding chapter I turn to a discussion of American policy toward Japan.

We hope that this volume, by bringing together the writings of Japanese and American scholars, will help further understanding of issues in the Japanese-American relationship. Such understanding is essential if the relationship is going to be mutually satisfactory and if it is to contribute to peace in Asia.

1. Toward a New Era in Japanese-American Relations

FUJI KAMIYA

THE DEBATE ON THE SEVENTIES

The closing months of the decade of the sixties have produced a wide-ranging debate on what can be expected in international politics in the world of the seventies. One reason for the intensity of this debate in Japan is public concern with such important issues as Okinawan reversion, the continuation of the U.S.-Japan Security Treaty and the Vietnam War. But in addition to concern with these crucial issues, all of which are making simultaneous demands for public attention, there is a general feeling that the world is entering into a major transitional period; that it is passing out of the "postwar" period and moving toward a new era. It is only natural that concern be focused on the prospects for this "coming age."

Moreover, the way in which the postwar era is coming to an end—the extreme radical anti-Communist Party leftist student movement in Japan and American frustrations over the Vietnam War are but two examples—has been so dramatic as to make us feel that in trying to gaze into the coming era we are peering into a dark and bottomless pit. "Futurology," despite its recent popularity, has not yet been able to quiet our fears and anxieties. But time will not wait for us to overcome our uneasiness. There is no way to avoid looking into the darkness that is the new era forcing itself upon us. All we can hope to do is slowly and carefully decipher its shape and try to minimize mistakes in dealing with it. It is this desire that has motivated the debate on the world of the seventies.

The subject of Japanese-American relations in the seventies is particularly difficult to deal with. One reason for this is the enormous changes that have occurred within Japan and the United States over the twenty-five years since the end of the Pacific War. The magnitude of change has been extraordinary. In Japan, for example, there is the contrast between the fear of mass starvation less than twenty-five years ago and the reality of having the third largest economy in the world today, in terms of gross national product. In the United States one has the bitter contrast between the successful landing of men on the moon and the frustrations produced by America's experience in Vietnam.

A second reason is the danger that Okinawa and economic relations, issues in the relationship demanding prompt solution, may become the source of emotional and irrational reactions. Because the Okinawa problem was ignored through much of the sixties and also because of the rapid changes in the position of Japan and the United States in the world economy in the same period, there is now a growing tendency to forsake rational discussion of problems for an emotional confrontation that exhibits mutual dissatisfaction and distrust. The possibility of such irrationality increasing in the future thus further complicates the relationship.

A third factor that makes looking into the future of the Japanese-American relationship so difficult is the reexamination in 1970 of the U.S.-Japan Security Treaty, a treaty that is at the heart of the distrust and dissatisfaction mentioned above. The Security Treaty issue is particularly complicated because it is often used as a way for Japanese to vent their national emotions and not as often considered in terms of how it relates to Japanese national interests. Some people in Japan look upon the Security Treaty as the source of all evil, much as philosophers during the Enlightenment viewed the monarchy and as Marxists regard capitalism. This view, having been reinforced by the escalation of the war in Vietnam and the exposure of evils in American society, has permeated public opinion and generated a general mood among the public.

On the other hand, the argument in the United States that the Security Treaty is giving Japan a "free ride," an argument that sums up the dissatisfaction and distrust felt by some people in the United States toward the Japanese-American relationship, has been rapidly gaining renewed strength. This argument reflects an emotionalism and irrationality as great if not greater than that exhibited by Japanese.

Fourth, there is the problem of grasping the importance for international politics of the seriousness of the domestic situation in both Japan and the United States. There are many differences in the specific domestic problems faced by Japan and the United States, but for both countries domestic issues are going to be extremely crucial and complicated, and political leaders will face great problems in trying to deal with them during the transitional period toward a new era.

As long as national goals are simply increased affluence and development, no matter how ambitious these goals may be, they can be handled within a framework of rational planning and forecasting. But when the social system and the principles and values underlying it are themselves brought into question, efforts to stabilize the system in a constructive manner cannot easily be made within traditional boundaries of planning and forecasting. Although President Nixon raised the cry of "law and order" during the Presidential campaign, since coming to office he has been able to do virtually nothing about this issue and has concentrated almost entirely on foreign policy. The Sato Administration, aware that university disputes would become nationwide, was at a loss as to how to deal with the problem, and finally railroaded through an unsatisfactory University Law. In short, although Japanese and American leaders recognize that they face the greatest challenges in the domestic area, they are at a loss as to how to cope with them.

The greater their inability to cope with domestic problems, the more political leaders try to shift attention to foreign policy issues. That this tendency is not restricted to the government or ruling party is, in Japan's case, clearly shown in the behavior of the Socialist Party.

The consequence of all of this is a tendency for foreign policy issues and issues in the Japanese-American relationship to be blown up out of proportion. An overloaded fuse is destroyed not because the fuse is defective but because the current is too strong. The danger of an analogous overload in the kind of attention given to Japanese-United States relations in the '70s adds to the complexity of anticipating future developments in the relationship.

Japanese-American relations in the coming years cannot escape these difficulties. Other problems, such as differences in cultural patterns and values, may further complicate the relationship and create discord. But as long as the long-range interests of the countries in seeking Asian security and development are the same, we must figure out a way to stabilize our relationship.

Resurgent nationalism in Japan will increasingly demand greater Japanese independence in foreign policy and will become increasingly less hesitant about competing with the United States. Forward-looking independence in the 1970s, however, cannot but be independence by interdependence. Since the end of the Pacific War relations between the United States and Japan have been characterized by the unequal relationship of guardian and protege. The time has now come to end that relationship and create a new interdependence based on a respect for independence. For the reasons mentioned above, creating such a new relationship will not be easy. Nonetheless it is incumbent upon us to make the attempt.

JAPAN'S INTERNATIONAL ENVIRONMENT

Let us turn to the international factors which will affect

Japanese-American relations in the 1970s. Because the rate of change is so fast in today's world, we can only hope to forecast events over a five to six year period at best. In the following sections, I will be dealing chiefly with the first half of the '70s, years of preparation and adjustment as I see it, to complete the transition into a new era.

First of all, peaceful coexistence between the United States and the Soviet Union, the biggest legacy of the post-war period, can be expected to continue during the 1970s. Despite verbal tirades exchanged between the United States and the Soviet Union over the Vietnam War, both nations recognize that peaceful coexistence is essential to the pursuit of their worldwide policies.

The development of new weapon technologies, such as MIRV missiles and the ABM can conceivably swing the nuclear balance of power between the United States and the Soviet Union to give one of them superiority. However, the mutual benefit in maintaining the present nuclear balance is recognized by both.

In addition, economic conditions in both nations make it difficult to persist in an unrestricted arms race. While each country will try to use the Chinese nuclear threat for its own purposes, both will probably work out a compromise with each other and conclude an agreement for nuclear arms limitation during the first half of the 1970s.

The gap between the U.S.-USSR position and that of secondary nuclear nations will only grow wider during the 70s. A decade of the de Gaulle Administration has proven that secondary nuclear powers like France and England cannot be of much military or political significance in the present world, and that the price for membership in the nuclear club is enormous economic hardship. Therefore it is likely that no country will attempt to become the sixth nuclear nation during the first half of the 1970s.

The Soviet Union is today facing enormous domestic and international problems. Like Japan and the United States, it appears to be going through a major transitional period.

Seventy-five communist parties participated in the World

Communist Party Congress held in Moscow in June, 1969.
But the invasion of Czechoslovakia and the dispute with
China have caused serious damage to the Soviet Union's
leadership position in the international Communist movement. One-half to two-thirds of the parties participating in
the Congress were of no major significance in international
politics, and no major Asian party participated. Secretary
Brezhnev suggested the possibility at the Congress of an
Asian Security Organization, a new concept in Soviet
foreign policy. It is unlikely, however, that this concept
will be translated into a concrete plan in the foreseeable
future. There is no reason to think that the Soviet Union
will be any more successful than the United States in
creating new and imaginative Asian policies, particularly in
light of the extremely complex and fluid international
situation in which it now finds itself.

It would appear that the difficulties the Soviet Union
finds itself confronting today will only reinforce the trend
towards greater cooperation with the United States. This
trend will be further strengthened, as is discussed below, by
a continuation of the Sino-Soviet split, a confrontation
which in all likelihood will persist and perhaps even worsen
in the coming years.

The lack of any expected major changes in relations
between the United States and the Soviet Union is a good
sign for Japan. It indicates that the international factors
which have sustained Japanese prosperity during the 1960s
will continue to be present.

CHINA

The succession of border incidents during 1969, such as
the Damansky Island incident in March and the Sinkiang-
Uigur Autonomous Region incidents in June and August
have further embittered Sino-Soviet relations. China now
refers to Soviet policies as "Socialist Imperialism" and
"New Czarism" and regards the USSR as China's current
major enemy. The Soviet Union for its part assumes that

China represents a real threat to its interest. Soviet pre-occupation with Chinese policy was clearly reflected in Brezhnev's speech at the World Communist Party Congress in June and Gromyko's report to the Supreme Soviet in July of 1969. As long as the conflict between China and the Soviet Union grows out of deeply entangled ideological and national interests, relations between these two states will not improve soon. In any event there is no likelihood for major improvement during the first half of the 1970s.

Adjustments in Sino-American and Sino-Japanese relations seem more probable than adjustments in Sino-Soviet relations. Though populated with more than seven times as many people as Japan, China is still economically weak. Its gross national product equals only about one-half of Japan's. Should this situation continue, China will have little ability, regardless of the tempo of its nuclear development, to qualify politically as the third-ranking nation in the world in the near future.

Because of these circumstances, China is likely to maintain a rather inflexible ideological line while at the same time taking practical steps to end its state of isolation. Also in the interest of countering the Soviet Union's aggressive policy in Asia, as exemplified in Soviet revision of policy toward Malaysia, naval deployment into the Indian Ocean, and its proposal for an Asian Security Organization, China will eventually conclude that it is undesirable to worsen relations with the United States or Japan.

But until China comes out of the throes of the Cultural Revolution with its use of slogans of American imperialism and Soviet revisionism as ideological weapons to mobilize domestic support, there is little likelihood that China will take any positive steps to improve relations with Japan and the United States.

THE KOREAN PENINSULA

Now, I would like to touch upon the outlook for developments in the Korean Peninsula in the 1970s, the land in which the policies of Japan, the United States, China and the Soviet Union crisscross, and a land with the most intimate relationship to Japanese security.

Turning our eyes first to North Korea, we find that the 1960s proved to be the first period of major economic slowdown for the Kim Il-song regime. Although the regime probably exaggerated the success of its first Five Year Plan of the latter half of the 1950s, claiming realization of the plan's goals in two and a half years and an average annual growth rate of 36.6%, this period undeniably was one of rapid economic growth. Politically as well, the Kim regime was able to stabilize its position, successfully overcoming an anti-Kim movement related to Khrushchev's rise to power and the criticism of Stalin.

Encouraged by these successes, Kim Il-song proposed a Seven-Year Economic Plan at the fourth Workers Party Congress, in September of 1961. But five years later he was forced to extend the Plan by three years, revamp the Party machinery, and carry out a series of massive purges. Kim Il-song attributed the disappointments of economic development in the early sixties to "the intensification of aggressive maneuvers by American imperialists for the past several years [which] has forced us to exert added efforts to strengthen our defense capabilities."[1] The real factors, however, were probably (1) a natural reaction against the rapid mobilization and development during the latter half of the 1950s; (2) misjudgment of the seriousness of the Sino-Soviet dispute and of Chinese national power; and (3) underestimation of the ability of the Pak regime, which came to power in 1961, to give new vitality to South Korea.

The so-called "autonomy, independence, and self-defense" line established by the North Korean regime during the sixties is probably more appropriate as a slogan for the seventies. More than anything else it demands the

[1] Report on the occasion of the 20th Founding Anniversary Conference in September of 1968.

establishment of strong internal leadership. The intensification of the movement to deify Kim Il-song since the purge of the Kapsan faction in 1967 has been encouraged for this reason. Intensification of guerrilla activities against the Republic of Korea since the Chonghwadae incident in January of 1968,[2] and the demonstration of its hard line against the United States in the Pueblo incident (January 1968), and the EC-121 incident (April 1969) have also been largely for domestic purposes. Viewed in another way, these activities may indicate that the Kim regime is not as strong and stable as it looks. The extended Seven Year Economic Plan will terminate in 1970, and North Korea will subsequently enter a new phase. But if our interpretation of the present situation is correct, the new line to be taken by North Korea during the 1970s, or at least during the first half of the decade, will emphasize recovery from the economic stagnation and political instability of the 1960s and preparation for a new leap forward.

Kim Il-song has persistently insisted that he will unite the Korean Peninsula "within our days" and "by any means necessary." It seems unlikely that the South Korean, North Korean, and international situations described by Kim as the three major elements in the quest for unification will combine in such a way as to lead him to make any positive moves. There may come a time when North Korea will shift from emphasis on domestic matters to a more positive approach in foreign affairs, but this will probably not occur at least until the latter half of the 1970s.

In South Korea, the Second Five-Year Plan will end in 1971, the year for the next presidential election. President Pak Chong-hi pushed through a revision of the Constitution allowing him to run for another term, despite widespread opposition. No one doubts that Pak will be re-elected, and the basic tone assumed by his third administration should not be too different from the basic policy of his second. In

[2] The attempted assassination of South Korean President Pak Chong-hi.

other words, the Republic of Korea will continue to emphasize economic growth and aim at surpassing North Korea economically. Consequently, the third Pak administration will emphasize strengthening its anti-guerilla defenses while shunning any aggressive approach to Korean unification.

On August 21 and 22, 1969, President Pak visited the United States and reached an agreement with President Nixon on the strengthening of U.S.-Korean joint defenses. The joint statement was not as hard-line as Korea might have wished. It avoided any commitment for new assistance and, on the whole, reflected careful consideration by the United States not to commit itself in the Korean Peninsula deeper than at present. Furthermore, as was indicated in the immediate cooperation extended by Soviet warships in the search for the shot-down American plane in the EC-121 incident, the Soviet Union also wants to maintain the *status quo* in the Korean Peninsula, for the time being at least. We can reasonably conclude that there is little probability for any drastic change in the Korean situation which would force Japan to make any sudden decisions on policy in the area. But for Japan simply to let this time go by would mean to lose a chance for readjusting policy that can never be recovered in the future.

STRAINS IN JAPANESE-AMERICAN RELATIONS

If changes in Japan's international environment conform to the above analysis, we can predict that there will be no radical changes in the first half of the seventies. It will be a period of transition and preparation.

If Japan and the United States successfully stabilize their relationship during this period, they will be able to meet the new Asian political situation of the latter half of the seventies with policies appropriate to their national interests and strengths. A failure to readjust the relationship will distort their policies in the entire Asian region.

The relations between Japan and the United States at

present give one the impression of a strained and deepening confrontation. Especially noteworthy is the "economic warfare" between the two countries. Over the past year or two, American statements on this problem have suddenly become harsh and edgy. The Anzai Economic Mission which visited the U.S. in April 1969 and the 6th U.S.-Japan Businessmen's Conference held in San Francisco in June reported an amazingly strong and emotional tone to speeches made by Americans.

The United States is presently taking every opportunity to express its dissatisfaction with Japanese restrictions on trade and capital liberalization. However, this situation did not develop overnight. It took many years before relations progressed to the present stage. But at no time in the past, even during the 1960s when Japan was enjoying very rapid growth, has the attitude of the United States been as harsh as now. This sudden and recent explosion of United States dissatisfaction has been precipitated by non-economic factors. In a nutshell, economic warfare seems to be not really economic, but political, warfare.

The reasons behind this suddenly increasing strain in U.S.-Japan economic relations for the past year are largely psychological. A comparison of the two nations' gross national products shows that America's exceeded Japan's by 14 times in 1955. Yet in 1968 this superiority was reduced to 6 times, and projection of current trends shows the gap reduced to 2.6 times by 1980.

Moreover, U.S.-Japan trade has been transformed from a U.S. surplus into a Japanese surplus since 1965. Japan registered a surplus of $1.1 billion in exports to the United States in 1968. Nevertheless, Japan places import restrictions on agricultural and other products and keeps automotive and certain other industries closed to foreign capital investment.

These problems go deeper than appears. In the background are American frustration with the Vietnam war, a feeling of crisis over the defense of the dollar, and a general uneasiness about America's international position and role

in Asia. While America's world position, both economic and
political, is suffering setbacks, Japan is steadily increasing
its international weight. And yet Japan, it seems to
Americans, goes on taking a stiff position on the Security
Treaty, American bases in Japan and the reversion of
Okinawa. It follows that what is really at issue is not
economic relations but much broader political and psychological questions relating to Japanese and Asian security.
In short, it is America's dissatisfaction with, anxiety about,
and distrust of Japan's overall foreign policy.

The Nixon administration has come onto the stage
seeking an end to the Vietnam war, the development of
new global policies after Vietnam, and the reunification of
America itself. But after a year of the Nixon administration, America is keenly aware that these problems are
indeed formidable. Nixon seems to be still groping for an
adequate approach to these problems. He does not seem to
have any clear conception for ending the Vietnam war,
which is prerequisite to diverting much energy to domestic
problems, and is now forced to promote a gradual de-
Americanization of the war. The only points he has scored
so far seem to be his diplomatic gestures to Rumania and
Hungary.

Thus America's dissatisfaction may focus solely on a
seemingly prosperous Japan. Japan is getting a "free ride"
on its security through the U.S.-Japan Security Treaty, is
taking advantage of America's Asian policies, is not bearing
a burden and responsibility commensurate with its economic might, and does nothing in this tumultuous era
except to exert every effort in negotiations with the United
States for the return of Okinawa.

If the frictions in the Japanese-American relationship are
due to a complex of political and psychological factors as
maintained above, it follows that they will not be removed
by agreements on trade and capital liberalization. What
would seem to be required is a change in Japan's overall
foreign policy. We cannot deny an element of justification
in America's emotional reaction to Japan, but the real task

facing the United States and Japan today is to re-examine their foreign policies in a calm and rational manner.

AMERICA'S TASKS

America's Asian policies during the postwar period have been based on a stereotyped view of the world as divided into "good guys" and "bad guys." Its cold war policies were based on a model of bi-polar conflict. Whether the major enemy was the Soviet Union in the 1950s or China in the 1960s, the stereotype has been maintained throughout. Now, however, America is being pressed to reconsider its rigid view of international politics in working out new policies in Asia.

Twenty years ago Owen Lattimore wrote that, "Ultimate general stability between America and Russia can be realized only upon their understanding that neither the United States nor Russia will be able to govern Asia completely. . .It is possible that Asia, now unmanageable by Western nations, can establish a new position in world politics through a series of landslides, causing massive tremblings but not enough to trigger general earthquakes." His outlook is in striking contrast to the cold-war policy which negates any Asian role and turns to outside threats in searching for the roots of instability in Asia. America, in search of new Asian policies for the 1970s, should replace the word "Russia" with "China" in Lattimore's passage and rethink its traditional approach.

What posture should we look for from the United States in playing a leading role in Asia as a Pacific nation? First of all, an overall strategy, integrating military and non-military aspects and maintaining an organic and appropriate equilibrium between the two, should be established. The question of Okinawan reversion is directly related to this issue. Viewed from a purely military point of view, the United States should quite naturally try to effect a reversion that would retain the *status quo* or as close to the *status quo* as possible concerning the use of military bases. However, viewed from an overall strategy, the emphasis has to be placed on balancing military disadvantages with political advantages. America's political judgment should identify America's national interests and goals in Asia during the decade of the 1970s, and a decision should be made on the importance of the role of Japanese-American relations therein, that is, the role both nations can play in achieving long-term stability in Asia through the stabilization of U.S.-Japan relations. Viewed from this strategic outlook, the return of Okinawa "by 1972, without nuclear weapons, and with the same base restrictions as in Japan proper" seems to have been the most appropriate agreement.

The same may be said about the termination of the Vietnam war. It looks quite certain that America will not realize her initial goal of making South Vietnam into a second Republic of Korea and keeping it within the free-world bloc. This, if viewed from narrow strategic standards based on a military approach, seems to be a major failure. However, viewed from the overall strategic standards, this has never been a goal worth attaining.

Secondly, there is in the United States today increasing criticism of the Defense Department and the military-industrial complex. On the other hand, the uniformed military men are trying to make a counterattack in order to regain ground lost during the reign of Secretary of Defense McNamara. There also is a confrontation between such foreign policy advisers as Henry Kissinger and Secretary of State Rogers, who take a more reformist posture, and those more conservative domestic policy makers. In the midst of a complicated and difficult situation, with these delicate and subtle confrontations present in addition to such great problems as race relations, urbanization, and student unrest, can President Nixon take the leadership in developing a comprehensive strategy for a multi-polarized Asia? The United States, for quite a long time, has been unable to show a quantitative, as well as qualitative, balance between its domestic and foreign policies.

Thirdly, the national objective of the United States in Asia in the 1970s will undergo a process of redefinition through America's recognition of Asia as a multipolar, not a bipolar, area. In this respect, it should be recognized that the function of any one nation in contributing to multipolar stability or a multilateral balance should naturally be different from that of others. Since World War Two the United States has only tried to obtain military cooperation, the right to use military bases, or participation in regional security systems, and has regarded the functions of different nations as differences merely in degree, not in kind.

Recently, strong American protests have been voiced that Japan is getting a "free ride" on the U.S.-Japan Security Treaty. However, this Treaty was originally intended as a free ride for Japan. In other words, since the United States did not accept the idea of a division of functions between nations, it let Japan ride free on military arrangements, but asked that Japan remain subservient and a ward of the United States. As the argument that Japan is riding free on the U.S.-Japan Security Treaty becomes increasingly vociferous, some people maintain that Japan should pay for its ride in the "same currency." As long as there is no marked change in the international situation or the basic relationship between the United States and Japan, Japan will continue in the 1970s not to have as much military power as many think is appropriate to Japan's economic power. At the same time, Japan is groping for a way to contribute actively to Asian economic development and political stability. This Japanese approach to the problem will not be realized as long as the United States is unable to understand the idea of different functions being performed by the United States and Japan. The question is how far the United States can accept "unique" and "ir-regular" participation by other nations, in spite of the fact that both Japan and the United States are economically and technologically advanced.

It is only natural that there be a basic difference

between the United States and Asian nations concerning their national objectives and ways of contributing to Asian peace and security. Korea wants the United States to maintain a cold war posture. Indonesia strongly demands assistance from the United States with no military strings attached. Cambodia is strongly neutral and regards even America's assistance and advice with suspicion. Considering these circumstances, efforts to formulate and enforce a single comprehensive strategy which can be applied to all Asian nations in the 1970s must be destined to fail from the beginning. Therefore, in view of differences between Asian nations concerning their interests, objectives, functions, and responsibilities, the United States should formulate several alternative policies, any one of which can be selected depending upon the situation. To what extent is America able to accept these kinds of differences? From the Monroe to the McNamara Doctrine, the traditional American policy has been to reduce all policies to doctrine or principle which could be upheld and treated with the strictness and vigor of a crusade. For better or worse, the United States adopted this doctrine successfully in postwar Europe. To what extent can America control the self-confidence gained from its European experiences in dealing with Asia?

JAPAN'S TASKS

Japan has become increasingly powerful economically in recent years and more self-confident, and this, along with the rise of a young generation, has led to stronger assertions of nationalism. Since the War, Japan has been influenced too heavily by the United States, whether favorably or not. Therefore, Japanese, especially the young, are trying to seek new and fresh sources of influence from other countries. It is increasingly believed that Japan can achieve independence and identity only by being liberated from American influence. This new version of nationalism, as well as a pacifism which has been widely supported since the War, controls the present mood of the Japanese people. If we analyze this mood a little more, we find not a true sense of independence and identity but rather a retrogressive anti-American tendency similar to an old, self-centered nationalism not oriented toward the pursuit of one's national interests in the broader sense. Independence here is something similar to escapism, a way to evade responsibilities in the international community.

The first half of the decade of the 1970s will be a preparatory stage for Japan to get ready to contribute actively in the latter half of the decade. At the same time, as I have mentioned previously, this is also a period for readjusting Japanese-American relations. If the above predictions of the international situation as it relates to Japan proves to be not too far from the truth, we could benefit from the valuable period of preparation. However, we could lose this opportunity if we do not have a clear vision of Japan's role in the Asia of the 1970s. The postwar tradition makes us Japanese belittle military power and stress the importance of economic strength. In a sense this is to be applauded, but it has also blinded us to the role of military strength in international politics. While one great power found it difficult to control Vietnamese nationalism in a corner of Southeast Asia, the military power of the other great power was successful in its suppression of Czechoslovak nationalism in Europe. For many years, South and North Korean troops have been confronting each other in the middle of the Korean Peninsula. It is impossible to discuss our long-term policies for security without reference to this fact. What is to be criticized about Japanese policy is not its emphasis on the use of non-military means to influence international politics but the tendency to believe that this approach is somehow easy, and to ignore the difficulties inherent in trying to effect a new approach to international involvement.

The most important area for Japanese-American security in the 1970s outside of the two countries themselves is, of course, the Korean Peninsula. Japan is greatly concerned about the stability of the peninsula, but does not, and must not, contribute directly to it in a military sense. On the other hand, Japan exports $600 million a year to South Korea, while South Korean exports to Japan amount to $100 million. This $500 million gap may be said to be actually subsidized by U.S. assistance to Korea. In the meantime, the U.S. stations two divisions there and contributes militarily to the security of that country. Looking at this from the American side, despite gradually increasing Japanese aid to Korea, it is perhaps natural for Americans to feel dissatisfaction and complain that Japan takes advantage of U.S. military and economic efforts in Korea and seeks only its own selfish interests.

In some respects, the new Japanese nationalism contains strong elements of the privacy-centered view and petty economic-centered orientation which was the postwar current. At one extreme, we have this nationalism expressed as international "my-home-ism" and at the other extreme we lack understanding as to the limits of one country's independence in this period of interdependence. It will be fortunate for us if these two extreme views do not distort Japanese nationalism in the 1970s. How then can Japanese postwar pacifism be evaluated in relation to the problems of the 1970s?

Postwar pacifism can be characterized by such sayings as "not taking up arms," "not making war," "not possessing nuclear weapons," "not sending troops overseas," etc. It is a negative pacifism, always opposing something. If Japan's task in the 1970s is to do something for Asia rather than nothing, then Japan should not remain limited by such pacifism, but should come out from behind it into a more positive and active pacifism. If Japan is to take a positive part in sharing international responsibilities without militarism, it is necessary to design "something" and develop an independent policy to achieve it. Yet Japan is ill-prepared for this task, which not only requires an ability to plan and act as more than just a "substitute" America but also demands that we establish our own overall strategy as quickly as possible.

According to a recent *Yomiuri* survey, over 70% of the Japanese do not wish to have nuclear weapons, but over 30% (nearly 39% of males and nearly 43% of young people aged 20 to 24) predict that Japan will have nuclear arms within ten years. It will be fortunate for us if this gap between hope and prediction does not express militarism and negative pacifism, ultranationalism and international "my-home-ism," dependency on the United States and anti-American nationalism, or a lack of understanding of an active pacifism and creative internationalism which ought to guide Japanese policies in the 1970s. Judging from the present situation, there is little possibility that Japanese opinion may be united between these extremes, and it is this which causes one to fear for Japan in the coming era.

If this view is correct, the tendency to regard the U.S.-Japan Security Treaty as a symbol of evil, to attack and blame it emotionally and moodily without reasonably analyzing its function, is likely to increase. As long as the true problems remain in such unseen psychological factors as mood or emotion, it is very difficult to solve them. When we consider that American dissatisfactions also come from psychological factors and seek hasty solutions, we might well expect that the U.S.-Japan Security Treaty may have to be terminated in the near future. This does not mean to say that the Security Treaty should be made a scapegoat for all evils, but that in order to create a new stable relationship it may be necessary to abrogate the Treaty. Such a move may be very difficult and dangerous, but it seems inescapable if we are to maintain a friendly relationship in the coming era. Japan and the United States should quickly and rationally discuss their mutual interests and seek to create in a positive way a new security system for Asia rather than passively accepting the continuation of a treaty that increases discontent and distrust on both sides. In this sense the first half of the 1970s should be used for laying the framework for a truly new and mutually satisfactory relationship.

2. The United States and Japan in the 1970s

MARIUS B. JANSEN

REDEFINING THE RELATIONSHIP

As the decade of the seventies begins, there is no reason to question the assumption that Japanese-American relations are in for redefinition and reformulation. The manner and the content of the decisions that are reached in the months ahead will determine the course of affairs between the two great Pacific powers for a good many years. On the American side a rising concern with domestic needs and disillusion with unilateral efforts at peace keeping combine with an awareness of Japan's wealth and power to produce the desire for greater Japanese involvement in Asia. On the Japanese side a new sense of power and confidence produces the desire for more autonomy, accompanied by the conviction of a less polarized world and consequently of greater choice. The long-standing hesitation to become an agent in enforcing American views of Pacific security is reinforced by a stronger consciousness of the need for world markets and the desire for world standing. Thus the assumptions of the recent past cannot be maintained on either side; Americans can no longer take Japan for granted, and Japan can no longer be as sure of having American protection on its own terms.

But one does well to stress the terms "redefinition" and "reformulation." Since World War II there has often been an undertone in much that has been written to suggest that there was something transitory and impermanent in the close ties between Japan and the United States, and a suggestion that the present arrangements were artificial ones made necessary and possible by the hostility of China. Writers in both Japan and America sometimes seem to think that either country has a more natural tie with the mainland. Japan's historic ties with China, and America's friendship for China, are assumed to constitute more natural links for the future. All of this is related to the alarm that greets suggestions of Japanese advances to China, and the fear of some Tokyo writers that the United States is somehow less bound to its China policy than is Japan. The Tokyo story of the Japanese ambassador to Washington who had nightmares about the United States recognizing Peking is a case in point.

I do not hold this view, and I do not even think that it is necessary to spend very long arguing against it. Japan's relations with China during her century of modernization have been so rocky that the present "abnormality" of separation marks an almost unprecedented period of peace. The China problem was consistently unsettling for modern Japanese internal politics. Arguments about the proper attitude to maintain toward the mainland neighbor provided focus for much of the rancor of politics, and in the years after World War I Chinese disunity and dangers of Chinese radicalism led directly to the disastrous course of Japanese militaristic diplomacy. Prewar economic relations between Japan and China, which took shape in an era of gross inequality between the contracting parties, also have little to tell about the ties that are possible in an era of equal competition. And the practical importance of cultural relations and shared experience diminish with each day that sees Japanese modernization leave its Asian neighbors farther behind, and with each student generation, on both sides, that learns fewer Chinese characters and less about traditional Chinese civilization.

The case is even weaker when it comes to Chinese-American ties. It could be argued, as some have, that the

American hiatus of relations with Japan was the "abnormal" interlude, and that both the extremes of enmity for Japan and sponsorship of China were products of highly special circumstances that interrupted a long-term development in which the American-Japanese relationships were of greater importance. Certainly in terms of the decade that lies ahead the shared experience, economic interests, industrial division of labor, and political and security goals that bind are between Japan and America. The friendship of each must be the other's single greatest concern in its Pacific policy. Both are *status quo* powers, with major concern for the continuation and improvement of the post war pattern, not its overturn. And when the argument shifts to cultural and social complementarity there is much to the recent argument of the Japanese sociologist Hidetoshi Kato. Only Japan and America, he writes, have passed through "modernization" to what he calls "contemporarization." Only these two have produced mass consumption societies motored by goals of constant upward mobility, regulated and stimulated by the mass media, their youth educated in mass higher education, and their values blended in the first mass homogenization of goals and tastes that the world has known. If similarity makes for complementarity and association, theirs is the "logical" relationship, and not that of either with the Chinese mainland.

The process of redefinition is not going to be easy. Japan's re-emergence began with American help, and American influence has been omnipresent. "Autonomy," "independence," "initiative," things Americans profess they want the Japanese to show, all gain meaning and conviction as they are exercised away from, or against, the United States' desires. It is hard to transform a patronage into a partnership when the preponderance of power has been so uneven. Nor is either side particularly good at thinking in terms of real partnership and equality. When the chips are down most Americans are going to remember that Japan owes a good deal of its strength and safety to their help.

The Japanese tradition and world view does not have very much room for equal partnership either. Feudal Japanese society was structured hierarchically, and if you were not above your counterpart you were probably below him. One finds it put perfectly in the admonition the great Meiji era diplomat Munemitsu Mutsu, the architect of Japan's rise to power in the 1890s, gave his son. "Do not," he wrote, "deal with people on a basis of equality. If you cannot patronize them, then let them patronize you." Japanese of the 1970s know a world very different from the feudal society into which Mutsu was born, but I suspect that there is enough of this view left to help account for Japan's remarkable patience in accepting a "low posture" role in world affairs.

Perhaps we should talk in terms of alliance rather than of partnership. Alliances can serve the contracting parties in different ways, as the Security Pact has served Japan and America. In an earlier day, the Anglo-Japanese alliance, under which Japan attained the status of a world power under the protection of the British fleet, was given broad construction when it suited Japanese purpose, narrow construction when it did not.

The areas of shared interests and values that tie the United States and Japan together are sufficiently pervasive to provide the basis for an alliance that will continue to serve both parties well. But both parties are going to construe their interests and their obligations differently at times, and an overall reckoning of cost and gain will be possible only in a survey sufficiently general to take account of what the costs or efforts would have been without the other's help.

There are reasons for thinking that the major determinants of the next stage of American-Japanese relations lie in Japan. These assertions can be qualified and debated, but the present level of interaction is probably more nearly to American than to Japanese satisfaction. United States leverage in the negotiations at hand is relatively limited. American pressures to increase Japanese participation and cost-sharing would probably be self-defeating and counter-productive. Real leverage could be exerted only through major negative decisions. One such would be a substantial withdrawal from present security commitments, and a second could be phrased in terms of economic protectionism. I will leave the exploration of these possibilities for others more qualified to treat them, except to say that I do not think thoroughgoing steps in either direction are likely. Moves against Japanese imports are likely to be piecemeal and not decisive; the pattern of economic inter-relationships is now sufficiently complex to contain its own safeguards and defenses. And a withdrawal so sweeping as to constitute a crisis for Japanese decision would probably hasten Japan's development as a nuclear power and thereby defeat or rule out other aims of American policy.

If, then, the principal incentives to change lie within Japan, they need to be considered in the convergence of generational and attitudinal changes that seek for Japan a new, larger, and more meaningful role. This is not an altogether new phenomenon in Japanese history, and it may be useful to examine some earlier cases to see if they have anything to contribute.

THE HISTORICAL PERSPECTIVE

A colleague once told me that Frank Lloyd Wright, when he learned he was an historian, snorted in contempt and asked whether his house faced backward as well. It is no doubt true that tradition tells us little about the course events will take, but it does contain continuities of style and emphasis, areas in which Wright, too, found much of interest in Japan. It seems to me that there are two precedents for the generational change in which Japan now finds itself, as well as several larger and more inclusive considerations of political and intellectual style.

This is not the first time a generation of young Japanese has tried to find meaning and mission after several decades of tumultuous change. The Meiji Restoration of 1868

brought with it many of the problems of identity that
followed the MacArthur Revolution, and they were not
resolved until the early 1890s, a quarter century after the
overthrow of Tokugawa feudalism. The high tide of
westernization came in the 1880s. During that decade
"Eastern" and "Oriental" seemed permanently pejorative
terms for weakness and backwardness. In a famous editorial, the journalist and educator Yukichi Fukuzawa called
on his countrymen to "part with Asia" on the grounds that
"if we keep bad company we get a bad name," and others
of his contemporaries wrote of "ridding ourselves of
Oriental traits." By the late 1880s a group of young
intellectuals set out to find meaning and role for their
country. Journals with names like *Japan* and *Japan and the
Japanese* posed the question, "How can Japan be made
Japan again?" Gradually the pendulum returned from
extremes of the Westernization to new emphases on
national spirit, national values, and national duty. Widespread popular irritation rose with the refusal of the treaty
powers to give modernizing Japan its due. The imperialist
West was slow to revise the "unequal treaties" that limited
Japan's autonomy and sovereignty. They also threatened
adjacent countries that seemed properly Japan's sphere. All
this combined to give point to a wave of nationalism that
followed the self-abasement of the 1880s. The early 1890s
saw the framework of Imperial Japan in place. The Constitution and Education Rescript came in 1890; revision of
the "unequal treaties" by Foreign Minister Mutsu followed
in 1894; and in 1895 Japan's victory over Manchu China
completed the process. As a popular journalist put it, that
victory sufficed "to dispel all previous misconceptions
about Japan's position in the world." Self doubt changed
almost overnight to self affirmation, and the support of the
young was guaranteed for their modernizing government.

Today the time span that separates young Japanese from
the wartime society of their fathers is about the same. The
old society, with its forced draft patriotism and militaristic
constraints, is substantially as foreign to them as Tokugawa

feudalism was to the Meiji generation. The interval of self-doubt and self-abasement through which they have passed was as total as the distaste the Meiji generation felt for its feudal past. But the differences are real and probably more important. Post-war Japanese society surely owes greatly to the civilian business-bureaucratic sector of pre-war Japan, and its dynamics have been more internal, its goals less derivative and imported than was the case with Meiji Westernization. True, many young Japanese have grown up conscious of their conquerors and tired of the security arrangements that seem to perpetuate some of the aspects of occupation. But while this represents "inequality" of a sort, it has gradually been transformed into an alliance with the world's strongest and wealthiest power, thus representing a far less galling situation than the Meiji treaties that subjected Japan to every Western power.[1] More particularly, the last decade of Japan's economic growth has found it the envy of much of the world, basking in international favor instead of sulking in the diplomatic weakness the Meiji men felt in an age of power politics. More Japanese have felt they were "ahead" of international styles and concerns in having left expensive nationalism behind them than were worried about falling behind in some new kind of power race. It is true that there is nothing in the Japanese tradition to suggest the Japanese will forever swear off power and accept anything less than the upper rungs. But Meiji history is probably a poor guide to the present situation.

Young Japan does not know very much about its father's generation, and it has no direct recollection of war, defeat and humiliation. But it is aware that the old style nationalism led to disaster. It is true that it is not surrounded with

[1](Note the comment of Dr. Nobumoto Ohama, in *Bungei Shunju* of April 1969: "American rule for 24 years is certainly too long, but things in this world have both bright and dark aspects...Okinawans have been ruled not by an inferior country, but by those who have self-confidence that they are one step ahead of others in civilization. From a long-range historical viewpoint, isn't this a revolutionary event for Okinawa...?" U.S. Embassy, *Summaries of Selected Japanese Magazines*, March 24-31, 1969, p. 22.)

scorn the way it was in the 1950s. Popular films now restore some of the villains of the 1930s to hero status, and publishers find a ready market for books and articles that remind their readers of the dreams of Asian leadership of prewar years. The nationalistic past begins to be suffused with a softer light, often one of romantic admiration for a simpler and more heroic time. Still, the nationalism of that past grew on the confusions of a pre-nationalist Asia, and it was fueled by a school-spread value system that substituted national for personal gratification. In the nationalistic Asia of today, in which both Koreas, both Chinas, both Viet Nams, India, Pakistan, and Indonesia shoulder staggering defense costs, there is little to tempt the political involvement of an insular Japan that feels itself unthreatened. Japan's post-war ethos has substituted economic for political, and personal for national, gratification so consistently that the internal dynamics of Meiji nationalist ambitions are lacking.

There is a second precedent that deserves a word. In the 1930s, a quarter century after the death of the Meiji Emperor and the departure of his ministers, another generation, one that never knew the weakness its elders had endured, and one that was trained in loyalty and convinced of national superiority, entered the paths of militarism and ultranationalism that led to Pearl Harbor and Hiroshima. A decade and more of progress toward political party rule, under business auspices, and a period of widespread enthusiasm for Western, and especially American, cultural forms, was abandoned in a drive for military greatness. The memory of Weimar Germany is always present. And the disciplined irrationality of the student shock troops in Tokyo contains enough reminders of the anarchistic aspects of the outlook of the young militarists in the early 1930s to make one pause. Shintaro Ishihara, writing shortly after the Shinjuku violence of October 1968, noted that "When you ask (students) what's to come of it, they reply, 'We don't know. But why should we know—someone will do it. At any rate, our mission is, before that, to cause great disorder and confusion in society!' "[2] It is impossible for me to read this without recalling the testimony of one of the young officers who murdered Premier Inukai in 1932. "We thought about destruction first," he explained. "We never considered taking on the duty of construction. We foresaw, however, that once the destruction was accomplished, somebody would take charge of construction."

These similarities of style are too striking to be overlooked. When we come to matters of substance, however, it is apparent that the preconditions for the militarist upsurge of the 1930s were very special. They included a collapse of the world economic and international systems. Japan suffered from the first and made important contributions to the second, but both were world phenomena. Further, there were two major elements of fear involved. The first was the Japanese alarm at the extension of revolutionary radicalism from China to Manchuria. A second was the conviction of the military that with the speed of Russian rearmament and industrialization the scales were swinging against Japan. Military planners worked against the deadline they foresaw in the "crisis of 1936," when the Soviet Union was scheduled to attain irreversible superiority.

Conceivably, economic and international systems could undergo change again and Japan could again feel threatened. But the most important contrast to the 1930s is that the structure of institutional power at that time favored the military. The gains of the 1920s had never been institutionalized or incorporated in theory or doctrine. Contemporary Japan, on the other hand, has important institutional safeguards against such a recurrence. There is no powerful military establishment. The Self Defense Establishment, if it has a political preference, has yet to demonstrate it. One should probably postulate some sort of conservative reaction against continued left and especially student

[2]U.S. Embassy, *Summaries of Selected Japanese Magazines*, November 18-25, 1968. From *Shukan Gendai*, November 14, 1968.

radicalism, in Japan as in America. But so far the caution of the Japanese government in international affairs has been paralleled by its hesitancy in provoking confrontations at home. And, finally, it is difficult to imagine the success of the military in the 1930s without their ability to embroil and commit the nation abroad. External involvements of a Manchurian type are no longer possible.

My conclusion from this excursion into Japan's recent history is that the precedents that have been cited are more interesting for the contrasts they contain than for the comparisons they offer. On the other hand, certain continuities of style are rather impressive. They concern matters of psychology and belief more than they do institutions. Consequently they bear on attitudes one might expect to see surface if there were a partial or total breakdown of the system that now flourishes.

Consideration of these begins with the frequently-expressed feeling of dissatisfaction with the performance of the partnership between big business and the political party that runs Japan. Impressively as it has worked and works, it has nevertheless failed to gain full legitimacy. Like Americans, Japanese are more successful in working things out in practice than they are in working them out in theory. "Theory" has been based upon absolute standards of rectity, purity, and sincerity. And since politics and business are necessarily imperfect, they seldom measure up. Nor could they, when the standards are set in impressively phrased, non-analytical, and frequently aesthetic terminology instead of in terms of process. One wonders at times whether the utilization of the Chinese writing system, with its heavy input of moralistic and Confucian vocabulary, may not have contributed to this escalation of political rectitude. In any case, Japan's present system cannot live up to the demands of democratic perfection postulated of it any more than the pre-war system was able to live up to the desire that it "show forth the true beauty of imperial rule," to cite a common phrasing of the goal. More even than Americans, Japanese have a built-in distaste for maneuvering, wheeling and dealing between interest groups. Their press rarely reflects the belief that a larger justice can be served by a process that brings competing political forces into balance by adroit politics. Dissatisfactions so engendered are of course charged against the government, for it is the only thing that can go wrong in a system in which "the people," as formerly "the emperor," are by definition good and deserving of better.

In Japan in 1969 one pole of this dissatisfaction was found in the student activists, who extended their condemnation of society to its entire capitalist structure, and, after linking it to America's, found it their duty to save their country from capitalist imperialism and their universities from serving as recruiting grounds for such iniquity. In demonstrating their sincerity and commitment they often benefit from the admiration of their countrymen who envy them their zeal, courage, and certitude even though their own positions may be very different. Thus the well-known rightist Yoshio Kodama, a veteran of every form of rightist extremism in the 1930s, was recently quoted to the effect that, while he thought the students were making a mistake, "when looking back upon my youth, I admit that youths have passions and violent emotions. They probably feel compelled to do what they do, at the sight of present politics, whether it's good or bad. Our right wing cannot go and clash with them on this." And, from a considerably different perspective, the establishment *Keizai Doyukai* (the Committee for Economic Development) was reported in the *Mainichi* of April 30 as charging the governing party with lacking a feeling of crisis, and showing a stagnant indifference to the "social needs of the people."[3]

Without this spectrum of agreement that there is something wrong and that the system needs repair, student radicals would of course meet less tolerance, in Japan as in America. But the case of Japan is more significant in the

[3]U.S. Embassy, *Summaries*, April 7-14, 1969, from *Shukan Asahi*, March 28, 1969; and *Mainichi*, April 30, 1969.

setting of tolerance of military activists in the 1930s, and of political activists—*shishi,* self-styled "men of high purpose"—in earlier days. In a crisis of doubt and limited participation, it requires only a small group of deeply, passionately, or joyously committed people to move the earth. The sport-club, recreational aspect of student extremism and routine deserves notice in this connection.

One might, in leaving the past, stop to note that students, comparable in numbers to the nineteenth century samurai, constitute the largest, most volatile, most committed, most urbanized, and most under-employed element in Japanese society. With a fine elite consciousness and scorn for the lower orders of class and morality which they disturb by their actions, they meet a mixture of tolerance, amusement and respect on the part of their fellow Japanese that has so far made them immune to discipline or reproof. Recent off-campus clashes, however, provide indications that this tolerance may be wearing thin.

PROSPECTS FOR JAPANESE POLICY

The larger past we have been talking about is probably not terribly important for the immediate future, where the constraints of the recent past operate. The expectations built up in the period since Japan's resumption of independence in 1952 provide the setting within which the decisions of the immediate future will fall. I assume in what follows that a reasonably satisfactory solution for reversion of Okinawa to Japanese rule is going to be reached between the two governments, and that June 1970 will find the Security Pact automatically continued and the Japanese-American tie still in being. Some sort of compromise may prove necessary on the use of Okinawan bases, possibly an informal arrangement somewhere between "free use" and "joint consultation." But I assume that the focus of the present agitation in Tokyo will gradually become indistinct.

Even so, it is very difficult to see very much movement

or change in Japanese policy during the short run period of a year or more which lies ahead. The constraints and continuities of Japan's recent policies are too great, and the pressures working against change of any proportion are too great. Japan's strategic dependence on the United States has been accompanied by the development of an extraordinary economic interdependence in which the United States provides one-third of Japan's trade and Japan provides one-tenth of America's. Although no formal peace treaty has been negotiated with the U.S.S.R., and issues of the northern islands await resolution, negotiations about trade and development find Japan with considerable ability to maneuver in the setting created by the Sino-Soviet split. Japan's relations with Communist China vary from faintly hopeful to disheartening, as at present; no formal relationship exists, and periodic hopes of trade advantages have so far run afoul of political and ideological upheavals. Those accompanying the recent Proletarian Cultural Revolution have served to confirm the caution with which Japanese leaders have viewed their country's relations with Peking. The tortuous negotiations of the last few months have found the "Memorandum Trade" with China much diminished, and Peking's hard line with Japanese exhibitions confirms once again the gloomy expectations of the China trade. For a brief period in 1966 Japan was the largest single trading partner of mainland China, and China briefly Japan's second most important export market. Hopes of renewal never die. But even in the period of peak growth the figures for trade with the United States were over ten times larger, they grew more rapidly, and they have been far more stable.

Relations with Taiwan and South Korea, meanwhile, have grown steadily. Like those with the mainland, they are supported by important interest groups within Japan. As Japan's need for additional labor grows, more and more functions are likely to be delegated to allied or branch firms in those countries. And Japan's recent participation in the Asia and Pacific Council (ASPAC), and her increased activity for development in Southeast Asia, show a gradual return to the international scene. Great care has been taken to limit that participation to economics and to avoid firm political commitments.

Quiet and inconspicuous as these activities have been, each of them has the support of a sector of Japanese opinion and politics, and each strengthens Japan's maneuverability with the others. It is important that Japan is taken up in, but not completely taken in by, each of several approaches to the world in which it lives. Out of this pattern of participation without commitment has come much greater autonomy than would otherwise have been the case. These policies have worked remarkably well, and by and large they have also served the interests of the United States, Japan's most important international contact. Purely on grounds of self-interest, there is little reason to expect Tokyo to entertain thoughts of radically increased commitment or investment in the immediate future.

The scene within Japan makes any such shift unlikely for the immediate future. The Japanese government is conveniently hemmed in by a number of restraints. The Peace Constitution, and Article 9, combine with the 1954 Diet Resolution against overseas use of Self Defense Force units to give force to a series of negative resolutions that are popular and seem compelling. One might compare them to the occasional "three anti" slogans of mainland China. Japan will not possess, not develop, and not permit the bringing in of nuclear weapons. Again, it does not possess nuclear weapons, it does not have military conscription, and it does not dispatch armed forces overseas. Article 9 of the Constitution, with its renunciation of war, can lead to extraordinary exchanges in the Diet, like the 1968 assurance of Security Agency Director General Masuda to the effect that the F4E Phantom, despite its attack capability, was not necessarily unconstitutional, since it was not planned to equip the planes with attack (bombing) devices. Or, as Kiichi Aichi suggested to an interviewer before his appointment as Foreign Minister in 1968, it should be possible, in view of Japan's high level of technology, to develop a type of plane which is "in keeping with the Japanese Constitution and with the people's sentiments, and which is still highly efficient." These are not sentiments that suggest an early turn to more dynamic or positive policies.

For the year to come the government's freedom of action is further limited by the wave of student activism that reached its height in 1969. In part this is a consequence of the speed of modernization which has brought to Japan all the overcrowding and underplanning that has afflicted other societies. The rate of students entering Japanese universities is now higher than the prewar rate of age group youths that entered middle school. Junior college, college, and university students today number 1,400,000, and faculties have not kept up with this expansion. In recent years a radicalization and fractionalization of the student movement has led to increasing violence, and since 1968 students have responded to elements of depersonalization in their university setting by depersonalizing their resistance. Masked, helmeted, and armed with staves and trained to toughness, they have resorted to guerrilla tactics in direct confrontation with special police units similarly garbed. Significantly, the police units carry large shields, symbolic of their essentially defense posture. Much of this movement has been specifically prepared for 1970, in the consciousness that the issues most successfully used for bridging factional disharmony are associated with opposition to the United States. As this is being written, the number of university campuses experiencing partial or total disruption of their activities has climbed to 94. Probably only the Cultural Revolution in China succeeded in bringing higher education to such a halt. Until measures are developed to deal with the students and reform the universities, it is difficult to imagine any government departing from the path of caution.

A third constraint upon the government's freedom of action is its political mandate. The conservatives have been more successful than was anticipated in most recent parliamentary elections, but they are still not likely to arrest or reverse the gradual erosion of the sweeping majorities they used to command in the countryside. The voters have left for the cities. The socialists are by no means heirs to their votes, and a more complex multi-party system may be in formation. But so long as there are no Yoshidas in sight able to cement factional unity, and in the absence of some spectacular accomplishment in international affairs, the government's dependence upon parliamentary support and allies is more likely to make for caution than for resolution. There is not in sight the kind of strong political leadership able to embrace or enforce unpopular alternatives. All the government's instincts, as one writer recently put it, caution it against positive policies that may cause dispute within its own party and give the opposition an issue.

Even with an Okinawan settlement, in other words, it is unlikely that the year 1970 will bring real changes. On the other hand, if the assumption of an Okinawan settlement proves mistaken, and if hopes now raised are sacrificed to American desires for full retention of discretionary use of Okinawan bases, one can be certain of a volume of bitterness and resentment that will fuel the student and other opposition groups more than anything we have seen so far. The costs to the government party, and certainly to Prime Minister Sato, would in all probability be permanent. And the carefully nurtured structure of American-Japanese cooperation and friendship might be the chief victim. Modern media have the capacity to transmit expressions of hate and irrationality with a directness and speed that guarantee their duplication in the receiver, and under such circumstances a series of reciprocal affronts could include violence at American bases, punitive protectionist proposals, and lasting harm to the intangibles of trust and friendship essential to an alliance between two great countries.

JAPAN'S WORLD ROLE

When we come to long range goals, the basic Japanese purpose will be one of achieving equality and consolidating autonomy. Japan is already a great power in all the ways that count, except in military strength. Even there, its power is by no means inconsiderable. The level of defense spending is about seventh in the world, as is Japan's population. It is out of line only in terms of Japan's enormous productivity. But even the present level of defense spending, assuming it is somewhat augmented to incorporate the responsibility of Okinawa and then kept proportional to GNP and budget, will make Japan a significant military power. Not, to be sure, in land forces, where the lack of conscription and insular security, combined with the naval weakness of her neighbors, make it unnecessary. But in the more expensive aspects of naval and air armament, Japan's technological superiority and economic potential over her Asian neighbors will give her maximum advantage. The forecast then is for forces that remain numerically modest by comparison to others in Asia, but more modern and better equipped.

Technological preparedness for nuclear developments makes this a possibility. A minister of cabinet ranks heads an atomic energy commission which supervises and coordinates research. Studies toward the application of nuclear power for ships and fuel are underway, and industry and medicine make increasing use of nuclear materials. In 1960 a Space Activities Council was set up to advance work in satellites and rockets; a launching and tracking center were set up, and meteorological rocket sales to Yugoslavia in 1959 and Indonesia in 1965 suggested the possibilities of military application. Government spokesmen have been emphatic in their assurance that nothing of the sort is projected. The examples of Britain, France, and China so far contain few arguments for the advocacy of the enormous investment nuclear development would require. Japan's conspicuous, self-proclaimed "pacifism" has been a useful, economical, and perhaps essential element in the development of her economic power. It would require either a new and vastly more pointed Chinese threat or a new and much more irritating American posture to produce popular approval of nuclear development. Polls show that popular sentiment has shifted in the direction of confidence that Japan "could" develop as a nuclear power if she so chose. A rising number of Japanese "expect" their country to do so in time, but so far there is little approval for such developments.

A drive for autonomy and equality among nations is in some ways the major continuity in Japan's hundred-year program of modernization. It precludes a docile or client relationship for more than the minimum period necessary. It raises the probability that the United States "model" will become less acceptable in terms of political leadership just at a time when it seems to become more relevant to Japanese society and economics than before. There is likely to be more interdependence, but less control.

Yet one must be very cautious about predictions of rising nationalism that base themselves on previous behavior and example. Certainly there are important nationalist ingredients in the student frenzy. Much of its rhetoric is execration, not glorification, of the Japanese social order, but that was true of the military theorists of the 1930s also. It is also true that Japanese today live in an expanded historical continuum in which more of the nationalism of the past is incorporated and justified. Writers like Fusao Hayashi see Japan's modernization as a hundred-year struggle for independence, a campaign in which the wars are little more than battles.

But allowance must also be made for the ways in which post-war Japan is post-nationalist in orientation. The effect of post-war education, and of most post-war experience, has been to reinforce the determination of 1945 that nationalism was a disaster. In recent years an extremely interesting dialogue has been carried on about the way and degree to which the nation should be valued, and refine-

ments of terminology agree overwhelmingly on the need to
avoid "nationalism" while permitting "patriotism" or,
better, "national consciousness." If all this means anything,
it surely means the abandonment of the old-style racist and
tribal superiority of the divinely favored nation.

Moreover, there is nowhere for a newly nationalistic
Japan to go in Asia. Its new-found, and again openly
admitted, superiority to its neighbors is one of modernity
and technology, and takes the form of refusing to focus on
Asia, and insisting on Japan's role as a world power and
trader. The old terminology and language of geopolitics
thus works poorly in the 1970s. Interdependence rules out
for Japan any thoughts of self-sufficiency or autarchy, and
a reasonably stable international system dominated by
super powers (that are likely, as George Ball reminds us in
the July 1969 *Foreign Affairs*, to remain super powers)
puts limitations on realistic formulations of autonomy and
equality.

Nevertheless, greater Japanese commitment is going to
become necessary. The Okinawan settlement is a prerequisite to smooth passage into the 1970s, but it is only
prerequisite and not a solution. Okinawan reversion in fact
solves nothing, and requires solutions. That is because a
good deal of Japan's pacifism has been premised upon and
made possible by the sacrifice of territory and nationals to
the American military administrators of Okinawa. A
number of recent magazine writers point out that
Okinawan reversion raises the question of whether it is
Okinawa that is to revert to Japan under terms of the
"three anti's," hitherto made possible by the separation of
Okinawa, or whether Japan is going to revert to Okinawa.
Does abstinence from military power become real through
the extension of the principle to Okinawa, or does return
of Okinawa force revelation of the emptiness of those
phrases? Any development that leads to nuclearization
would mean the latter. Special rights for the American
military would require a new security agreement with Japan
that would be certain to produce a rumpus in Tokyo. Even

reversion on homeland conditions, the Japanese government's announced goal, would bring with it requirements
for added conventional defense measures sufficient to incorporate the increase in territory under Japanese control.

The areas most likely to engage Japanese and American
attention in the next decade are political, and they will
center around issues of China, of security, and of development. I believe that the least troublesome of these will
concern China, for American and Japanese interests
probably do not conflict seriously there. Both countries
have reasons to hope for a reopening of China, with access
to its people, its markets, and its government. Both hope
for progress in modernization and development in China
that will lessen the willingness to take risks while producing
revisionist moderation. Both have an identical interest in
discouraging Chinese expansionism. Except for romantics in
both Japan and America, both sides have modest expectations of Chinese growth and development. China's priority
nuclear development, its population growth, and the consequences of its closed economic structure make rapid
growth unlikely. A survey by Kiichi Saeki in 1969 estimates that China may not have a second strike capacity
before 15-20 years. In five years China's GNP may be in
the area of 120 billion dollars. But Japan's, in that same
period, will pass 270 billion dollars, and it will probably be
as large as or larger than the total GNP of all other Asian
countries, including China.[4]

The same period is likely to see a changing of the guard
in Taipei as well as in Peking, and there is at least the
possibility of a shift to greater flexibility on the mainland.
Yet nothing is going to change the facts of China's handi-
caps in industrialization and modernization, her priorities,
or Japan's long head start. Japan's need for world trading
partners will increase rather than diminish, and there is

[4]"Role of Japan, Country Alien to Asia," *Jiyu* (March 1969), *Summaries of Selected Japanese Magazines*, March 24-31, 1969.

little reason to expect her to jeopardize any of this for momentary advantage with the Chinese mainland. On the whole, it will be in the American interest to encourage the Japanese to do what it will be impossible to prevent their doing—to experiment with ways of improving relations with Peking and to enlarge areas of trade.

Security problems, on the other hand, will involve both the Japanese conception of the world, and their interest in contributing toward the defense of others. Taiwan and South Korea will be especially important areas at issue. Although there is a good deal of disagreement on these points in some quarters in Tokyo, the present consensus would seem to be strongly with Mr. Saeki's assertion that an increase in Japan's military power in proportion to the pullout of United States military power would evoke a corresponding increase in the Soviet Union's and Communist China's military preparedness. These countries would consider such an increase as outside the boundaries of Japan's own defense concerns, requiring additional and futile efforts to maintain the balance of power at a higher level. Japan's support of resistance to aggression, he goes on, could not go beyond cooperation through provision of bases and logistics for American forces, and then only if the aggression took the form of "unmistakable military invasion." Japan's intervention, on the other hand, could only provoke counter intervention by the Soviet Union and Communist China, despite Japan's inability to hold such intervention in check. In short, he concludes, "there is little possibility of Japan's possessing such means [for intervention] in the near future by rewriting its Constitution. Nor is it conceivable that the foreseeable Asian situation will strongly demand that." These views, coming as they do from a leading strategic planner and "realist," command respect and remind us that not even an American "withdrawal" will guarantee a Japanese "entry."

A third area, and one in which Japan's contribution will be immediately requested and needed, is that of Asian development. Professor Wakaizumi has recently suggested that Japan could well double her spending on aid, with particular reference to the development of Asia, and increase her defense spending too. Americans at times make still more sweeping suggestions. Mr. Saeki also advocates more attention to development, but emphasizes its difficulties. Where the United States with its resources failed, he points out, Japan is not likely to succeed with less. He would build on strength rather than on weakness, and concentrate on the development of partly modernized areas like South Korea, Taiwan, Thailand, Singapore, and Malaysia, proceeding with greater caution in more difficult and less familiar countries.

Political problems will probably loom larger than economic problems in the relations between Japan and the United States in the 1970s. The economic problems and frictions to some degree cancel each other out, and it is seldom that one or a group become sufficiently persuasive to alter national policy. Yet it is also true that there is no true precedent for the kind of interrelationship that is now binding the two economies together, and this itself constitutes a major factor in the likelihood of continuing close cooperation.

This may probably be the first time that an essay on future Japanese relations has brought in the GNP this late in the discussion. In 1967 it stood at 120 billion dollars. It was about 140 billion in 1968, and is projected at 160 billion for 1969. By 1975 it will exceed those of the United Kingdom and France combined, even if the rate of growth slows. It will also, as has been mentioned, equal that of all of Asia including that of Communist China. In 1967 Japanese per capita production of crude steel, which totaled 62 million tons, was approximately the same as America's. Fuji-Yawata, the new steel giant, will probably overtake U.S. Steel as the world's largest producer by 1975. Bulk transport evens out the disadvantages of deficiencies of raw materials, while economic growth increases the need for imports like timber (which now stands second, after petroleum) and feed grains.

All of this commits Japan firmly to a world, rather than a regional, role. In world trade its position changes, worsening as wage rates rise and import needs go up but, at the same time, improving as rapid growth produces ever larger economies of scale as size of firm, breadth of market, and increment of know-how accumulate. These advantages are incremental and not transitional. From this is developing an international division of labor that meshes poorly with our usual categories of analysis in terms of nation states. Japan, as James Abegglen recently put it, builds America's ships, makes most of its electronic entertainment equipment, and may come to dominate in small cars and luxury compacts. The United States makes Japan's large computers, its aircraft, and will dominate in space industries, although even here patterns of subcontracting and division can develop. Thus a kind of interdependence develops that requires stretching of ways of thinking and speech and editorial writing.

In addition to sharing in developed markets where labor costs and technology give it the advantage, Japan is beginning to turn to less developed neighboring societies to share some of the functions it formerly performed itself. Many exports that were formerly Japanese have already shifted to Taiwan and Korea. Saburo Okita recently pointed out that Korea's export list today closely resembles Japan's of fifteen years ago. In 1966 Japan became a net importer of raw silk, and in 1967 of cotton yarn.

JAPAN'S DOMESTIC PROBLEMS

Changes of this magnitude are going to continue and accelerate in the 1970s. As they do they will provide obvious points of friction between Japan and other countries. But they also involve important problems of domestic adjustment that will operate to turn Japan inward, in the way that America is today concerned with its own problems. The scale of urbanization will accelerate. By 1975 the villages, long the strongholds of Japanese conservatism, will contain less than 20% of the country's population. The labor force will change to a high-quality, highly educated one, and the typical pattern of residence will become that of the urban or suburban multi-family unit, cramped in space and crowded with appliances.

Japan already has more cities of over one million population than the United States (7 to 5) and more cities of 100,000 to 1,000,000 (130 to 125). People are moving out of city centers, because of the shortage of land, but industries are not. The commuter pressure rises. Road building and automobile ownership increase rapidly, but because of geographic limitations it is more probable that this will operate to increase metropolitan activities (as the new Tokaido has operated to multiply the functions that can be carried out from Tokyo) rather than disperse them. Planning for this urban explosion is still poorly advanced. In terms of capital available, the public sector, given the modest per capita income (and tax yield), is relatively weaker than in the United States. Yet land prices in Tokyo run from five to 100 times those of the New York area, and the proportion of city space devoted to roads in Tokyo is a mere 10%, compared to 30% in New York and 55% in Los Angeles. Japan's unit cost for highways is the highest in the world. In a city in which an automobile requires 200 square feet for storage and the average new dwelling space per family is only twice that, it is clearly desirable to export virtually the entire automobile production. Only in the provision for public mass transport is the Japanese city ahead of its American counterpart. In every other aspect of social overhead it is well behind, and the assault on the Japanese environment is easily the equivalent of anything Americans know. Moreover, the development of company and government housing is beginning to produce the neighborhood stratified by income and class long familiar in the United States. School and other differentiations may thus be the next stage.

In other words, when it comes to conditions of life the GNP, while a precondition to solution of the problems

Japan faces, brings as many problems as it answers, just as reversion of Okinawa does for national security policies. It is concern for the quality and conditions of life that helps account for the misgivings of Japan's non-rioting student majority, and the charge of the *Keizai Doyukai* that the government is indifferent to "social needs." Economic growth thus guarantees that Japan will have to turn inward to face its own problems at the same time that it has to keep its lines open to all possible trading partners, above all to the United States.

Finally, the political setting in which these problems are played out is one in which the long-term decline of the once absolute conservative majorities will continue. The way in which the government reacts to the problems that have been sketched out will affect its longevity at every level. On the whole there is little that needs to be added to the political prospects discussed by Herbert Passin in The American Assembly's *The United States and Japan* in 1966,[5] except for several developments that should be noted.

The first is a revival of the strength of the Japanese Communist Party. Beginning in 1965, at a time when the American bombings of North Vietnam helped to radicalize the political scene, the JCP's public break with Peking cleared it of the charge of being a Chinese puppet. "Nationalism" and "autonomy" helped its image. But its long-term appeal has probably profited more from the charge levied against it by Maoist and Trotskyite student groups of being a part of the Japanese establishment. As anarchist and extremist student groups took to the streets, the JCP-related *Minseido* student organizations proved to be the campus "moderates" in case after case. In one major and celebrated case a university administration, in the name of university autonomy and academic freedom, even "armed" (with staves) a *Minseido* faction to help it oust an invading Maoist faction from the campus rather than call in the

---

[5]Herbert Passin, *The United States and Japan* (New Jersey, 1966), pp. 147ff.

police. As a result, the JCP-related organizations are in a
better position to control *Zengakuren* and campuses all
over Japan than they have ever been before. The organization has been expanding its activities to senior high schools,
and now claims chapters in one out of every five high
schools. This activity has yet to be translated into votes in
national elections, but one could imagine a setting in which
the Communist Party might become as significant an element
in the voting pattern as it is in France and Italy.

A second is the development by the *Komeito*, the
political arm of the *Soka Gakkai*, of a platform on international affairs. With a constituency of 25 in the lower, and
24 in the upper house of the Japanese Diet, the *Komeito*
is now a significant element in politics, and at least a
possibility to tie-up with the ruling conservatives if their
fortunes slip. It is then significant that the stand adopted at
the 7th annual convention in January, 1969, contains no
suggestion of endorsement for "positive" nationalist action,
but is instead a composite of every generalized aspiration of
leadership with safety, and spiritualism with profit, that has
appeared since World War II. The Security Pact with the
United States should be phased out during the 1970s,
beginning with elimination of unnecessary bases, and going
on to complete Japanese neutrality. Communist China
should be won over by taking a strong "one China" stand
and leaving Taiwan to "Chinese" solution. Japan is immune
to subversion so long as "we maintain a rich economic
power and enjoy a high living standard." China should be
sponsored for admission to the United Nations, and an
Asian headquarters of that organization should be established in Tokyo. The Self Defense Forces, now a unit in
the international American line-up, should be changed into
an autonomous National Guard with no other duty than to
resist invaders and maintain peace and order within Japan.
The organization which has adopted these "principles" is
often heralded as the advance agent of a new Japanese
nationalism. But its program here summarized is a pastiche
of the liberal-neutralist consensus of post-war Japan, and it

does not promise much support for a government anxious to undertake new positions in its external relations.

IN CONCLUSION

I come, then, to these conclusions:

First, the constraints of internal pressures and the recent past will combine to keep Japan from showing very much movement during the years immediately ahead.

Second, the content of the settlements now being negotiated, and the manner in which decisions are reached will be of critical importance for at least the next decade of Japanese-American relations. If nothing else, they will determine the form and direction of Japan's drive for autonomy and status. If the alliance proves to be a relatively comfortable one with sharing of decisions and responsibilities, as Okinawa reverts on a "homeland basis," then many more forms of consultation and cooperation will follow. Frustrations engendered in the negotiations, or anger roused by their results, however, could produce as the first consensus of post-war Japan a determination to prepare to go it alone complete with nuclear armament. Such a position could be compatible with the wishes of both right and left, and could be sold and advertised as neutralism.

Third, no dominant political grouping is in sight, nor is any consensus beyond that of "autonomy" likely to emerge. The likelihood therefore is for a continuation of the type of compromise and caution of recent years.

Fourth, the examples of past nationalism will continue to repel rather than to attract. Japan's participation in international events is likely to continue to show a caution reflecting a desire to avoid irreversible commitments in an Asia still unstable. Her contributions to economic development, however, should show significant increase.

Fifth, pressures and un-met needs that grow out of the pace of internal change will force the application of increasing amounts of capital and effort to tasks of domestic, especially urban, reform, for this will be the condition of continuance in office for any government.

Sixth, the mercurial nature of Japan's younger generation, and its dissatisfaction with the present goals and values of society, make it more than ordinarily important that the world, and especially the United States, not take Japan for granted. Pronounced slights from allies, or unusually brutal threats from neighbors, could yet swing the balance and permit a more highly fueled move to fully armed status in the international community. It is the task of statesmanship and the responsibility of opinion leaders in both countries to guard against contributing to such trends, lest correctable or adjustable vibrations become irreversible oscillations that do permanent harm to the present structure of Japanese-American relations.

3. GROWTH FOR WHAT?
The Issue of the 'Seventies
JAMES WILLIAM MORLEY

JAPAN, THE ECONOMIC GIANT

Last year Japan burst the European barrier to become the third largest economic power in the world after the United States and the Soviet Union. It was an event of world-wide significance. No one calls the Japanese "transistor salesmen" now! As Japan's scholars, businessmen, and government and political leaders travel about the world, their words and actions are now observed with some of the same rapt attention recently accorded the space explorers of the moon. For the world now wants to know: what role will this new Japanese giant carve out for itself? how will it use its vast new economic strength? to seek to enrich only itself? or to share its market with the rest of the world? to overwhelm its neighbors, to ignore them? or to help them solve their cultural, economic and security needs?

The Japanese people themselves are equally perplexed. For one hundred years they have had a monkey on their backs: the desire—no, it was stronger than that—the felt necessity to catch up with the West. In the prewar period it was the West's power that attracted, and all of the nation's

The paper was prepared during the author's service as Special Assistant to the United States Ambassador in Tokyo. It draws, however, primarily on his private, rather than his official, experience and should in no way be taken to represent the views of the United States Government.

energies were harnessed to trying to match and then overcome it. That effort having failed militarily, the Japanese
concentrated their efforts in the postwar period into new
channels of democratization and economic growth. Especially in recent years, economic growth has been pursued
with a single-minded devotion probably unprecedented in
the world, and that devotion has paid off handsomely. The
annual growth rate has averaged more than 16%, resulting
in a quadrupling of the GNP in just the past ten years. This
has produced a growth in GNP per capita at an annual rate
of 15.3% over the same period, raising that absolute
amount from less than $388 (140,000 yen) in 1959 to
approximately $1,399 (504,000 yen) in 1968.

Inevitably, the first question posed for the 1970s is, can
this prodigious rate of growth be sustained? A few years
ago, indeed up until a few months ago, few forecasters
would have said so. Most would have argued that 7 or 8
per cent (at constant prices) would be a realistic maximum.[1] But today the climate of opinion is shifting. The
experience of two decades of dramatic growth is breeding
confidence. The careful Japan Economic Research Center,
for example, recently estimated that for the years immediately ahead the rate may climb to a new average high of
16.7% (at current prices).[2] Even assuming that a brief
recession period such as has afflicted the Japanese economy
every three or four years in the past may lie ahead, the
Government of Japan, therefore, at least through the first
half of the 1970s, will be strongly pressed to pursue
policies designed to sustain the growth rate at somewhere
around its average of the past decade, aiming at an

---

[1] See, for example, the Economic Planning Board's target rates of 6.5% for
its 1958-62 long-range plan, 8.2% for the next, and 8.3% for the current plan
originally designed to cover 1967-71, but now undergoing review. See also, for
example, Herman Kahn and Anthony J. Wiener's forecasts of 5-9% in their *The
Year 2000* (New York: Macmillan, 1967), p. 159; and Hugh Patrick's forecast
of "at least 6-8%" in his "The Phoenix Risen From the Ashes: Postwar Japan,"
Center Discussion Paper No. 59, Economic Growth Center, Yale University,
mimeo, October 1968, p. 55.

[2] *Nihon Keizai*, July 15, 1969.

Table I — GROWTH IN GNP, 1950-1968

Calendar Year	GNP at Constant 1965 Prices			GNP at Current Prices			World Rank of GNP at Current Prices
	Billions of Yen	Billions of Yen (1)	% Change	Billions of Yen	Billions of Dollars (1)	% Change	
1959	17,257.7	47.9	9.2	12,926.3	35.9	12.2	6
1960	19,698.7	54.7	14.1	15,499.2	43.1	19.9	6
1961	22,765.9	63.2	15.6	19,125.5	53.1	23.4	6
1962	24,228.1	67.3	6.4	21,199.2	58.9	10.8	6
1963	26,785.3	74.4	10.6	24,464.0	68.0	15.4	6
1964	30,361.2	84.3	13.3	28,832.9	80.1	17.9	6
1965	31,713.9	88.1	4.5	31,792.9	88.3	10.2	6
1966	34,899.9	96.9	10.0	36,557.4	101.5	15.0	6
1967	39,403.1	109.5	12.9	43,038.9	119.6	17.7	4
1968	45,096.1	125.3	14.4	51,092.0	141.9	18.7	3
Average for ten years, 1959-1968:			11.1			16.1	

Source: Japanese Government, Economic Planning Agency

(1)   Converted at Y360.00 = $1.00

Table II – GROWTH IN GNP PER CAPITA, 1959-1968

Calendar Year	Population[1] (1,000)	World Rank of GNP Per Capita[2]	GNP Per Capita at Current Prices	
			Yen (1,000)	Dollars
1959	92,640		140	388
1960	93,420	21	166	461
1961	94,290		203	563
1962	95,180		223	619
1963	96,160		254	707
1964	97,180		297	824
1965	98,270	21	324	899
1966	99,050		369	1,025
1967	100,240		429	1,193
1968	101,408		504	1,399
Average annual increase:			15.3%	

1. Bureau of Statistics, Prime Minister's Office, *Monthly Statistics of Japan*, No.93, March 1969, p.3.

2. Japan Research Center estimates in *Nihon Keizai*, July 15, 1969.

3. In dollars at current prices, derived by dividing population estimate by GNP at current prices in billions of dollars for each corresponding year in Table I above.

expansion of the GNP by 1975 to $403.5 billion (145,270.8 billion yen) and the per capita GNP to $3,671 (1,322 thousand yen).

Such an objective will strongly justify those elements which favor a continued allocation of resources along the lines which have proved so successful in the recent past. This is a uniquely Japanese pattern characterized by relatively low consumption, low government expenditure (roughly 10% of GNP), and high private investment. On the other hand, the larger the economic pie becomes, the more urgent the demands from various quarters for a larger share of it. Eight of these demands will be particularly insistent in the 1970s. How Japan responds to them will largely determine its future growth, the quality of its life, and its role in the world.

LABOR'S DEMANDS

One pressure will be to increase the proportionate allocation for wages. With the rate of population growth holding steady at no more than about 1% a year, the GNP per capita has been rising rapidly, probably reaching a level this year of about $1,600 (See Table II). If the GNP continues to grow along the lines of the primary forecast above, the GNP per capita can be expected in 1975 to have more than doubled again, reaching a figure of more than $3,600, which is slightly higher than that in the United States in 1965 (See Table IV). Wages have risen rapidly, generally increasing at an annual rate of 9% or more (See Table IX); but, the 15.3% annual increase in the GNP per capita (See Table II) convinces the wage-earner that he is not getting his fair share. Management replies that the fault is labor's, noting that labor productivity over the same period increased at an annual average of only 7.5% (See Table X) so that wage increases at 9% are in fact raising costs disproportionately, thereby making a disproportionate demand on the economy's resources and pushing up prices to a dangerous degree.

Table III – A PRIMARY FORECAST OF GROWTH IN GNP, 1969-1975

Year	Average Annual % Change of GNP at Constant Prices, 1959-68 [1]	GNP at Constant 1965 Prices		Average Annual % Change of GNP at Current Prices, 1959-68 [1]	GNP at Current Prices	
		Billions of Yen	Billions of Dollars [2]		Billions of Yen	Billions of Dollars [2]
1969	11.1%	50,101.8	139.2	16.1	59,317.8	164.8
1970	11.1	55,693.1	154.7	16.1	68,868.0	191.3
1971	11.1	61,875.0	171.9	16.1	79,955.7	222.1
1972	11.1	68,743.1	191.0	16.1	92,828.6	257.9
1973	11.1	76,373.6	212.1	16.1	107,774.0	299.4
1974	11.1	84,851.1	235.7	16.1	125,125.6	347.6
1975	11.1	94,269.6	261.9	16.1	145,270.8	403.5

[1] From Table I above.

[2] Converted at Y 360.00 = $1.00.

Table IV – A PRIMARY FORECAST OF GROWTH IN GNP PER CAPITA, 1969-1975

Calendar Year	Population[1] (1,000)	GNP Per Capita at Current Prices[2]		World Rank of GNP Per Capita[3]	Comparison with U.S.	
		Yen (1,000)	Dollars		GNP Per Capita at Current Prices	Year
1969	102,569	578	1,607		$1,605[4]	1947
1970	103,744	664	1,844	17		
1971	104,929	762	2,117			
1972	106,140	874	2,430			
1973	107,372	1,004	2,788			
1974	108,635	1,152	3,200	9	3,520[4]	1965
1975	109,925	1,322	3,671		6,209[5]	1975

1 Ministry of Health and Welfare, Institute of Population Problems.

2 In dollars at current prices, derived by dividing population estimate by GNP at current prices in billions of dollars for each corresponding year in Table II above.

3 Japan Research Center estimates in *Nihon Keizai*, July 15, 1969.

4 In dollars at current prices, derived by dividing population estimate by GNP at current prices in billions of dollars, using data in U. S. Congress, Joint Economic Committee, *1967 Supplement to Economic Indicators* (GPO, Washington, D. C., 1967), p. 7, 15.

5 Japan Research Center estimate in *Nihon Keizai*, July 15, 1969.

Table V – JAPAN'S GNP AS PER CENT OF U. S. GNP, 1960-1975
Derived from data in Tables I-IV

Calendar Year	Total GNP	GNP Per Capita
1960	8.6%	16.5%
1965	12.9	25.6
	Primary Forecast	
1970	19.4	38.8
1975	30.6	59.1

Table VI – A COMPARISON OF GROSS NATIONAL EXPENDITURE OF JAPAN AND U.S., 1952-1967

Calendar Year	Total GNP		Personal Consumption		Gross Private Domestic Investment		Government Purchases		Net Exports	
	Japan	U.S.	Japan	U.S.	Japan	U.S.	Japan	U.S.	Japan	U.S.
	(Billion Dollars)		(Per Cent. of Total)		(Per Cent. of Total)		(Per Cent. of Total)		(Per Cent. of Total)	
1952	17.3	345.5	61.7	62.7	26.6	15.0	10.7	21.6	0.01	0.6
1957	30.8	441.1	58.4	63.8	34.5	15.4	9.0	19.5	-1.9	1.3
1962	58.0	560.3	54.7	63.4	36.6	14.8	8.7	20.9	-0.03	0.9
1967	115.5	789.7	52.7	62.3	38.3	14.5	9.0	22.6	-0.01	0.6
Average annual % change, 1952-1967:			-0.57		+0.38		0.0		+0.45	

Sources: U.S. GNP and percentages for 1952, 1957, 1962 calculated from data in U.S. Congress, Joint Economic Committee, *1967 Supplement to Economic Indicators* (GPO, Washington, D.C.), p. 7, and for 1967 from *Economic Indicators*, April 1969, p. 2.

Japanese GNP and percentages for 1952 calculated from data of National Income Section, Economic Research Institute, Economic Planning Agency, and for 1957, 1962, and 1967 from Bureau of Statistics, Office of the Prime Minister, *Monthly Statistics of Japan*, No. 93, March 1969, p. 117.

Table VII – NATIONAL BUDGET EXPENDITURES, 1962-1967

(in 1 million yen and %)

	FY 1962 (closed)		FY 1963 (closed)		FY 1964 (closed)		FY 1965 (closed)		FY 1966 (budget)		FY 1967 (original budget)	
	Amount	% total	Amount	% total	Amount	% total	Amount	% total	Amount	% total	Amount	% total
TOTAL	2,556,617	100.00	3,044,292	100.00	3,310,969	100.00	3,723,017	100.00	4,477,148	100.00	4,950,910	100.00
National Administration	220,879	8.64	259,047	8.51	289,431	8.74	330,777	8.88	329,924	7.37	366,513	7.40
Local Finance	489,056	19.13	586,815	19.28	639,652	19.32	720,067	19.34	837,262	18.70	923,128	18.65
National Defense	217,308	8.50	245,170	8.05	281,262	8.49	336,937	8.24	346,543	7.74	382,516	7.73
Foreign Obligations (incl. Reparations)	29,210	1.14	24,020	0.79	25,619	0.77	19,750	0.53	31,558	0.70	33,604	0.68
Land Conservation & Development	469,676	18.37	538,179	17.68	610,746	18.45	714,303	19.19	838,386	18.73	936,683	18.92
Industrial Development	188,816	7.39	217,264	7.14	266,528	8.05	337,802	8.27	513,701	11.47	452,180	9.13
Education & Culture	305,582	11.95	369,779	12.15	408,774	12.35	471,847	12.67	544,526	12.16	605,541	12.23
Social Security, etc.	369,330	14.45	453,898	14.91	517,001	15.61	640,211	17.20	735,341	16.42	836,306	16.89
Pensions	123,157	4.82	133,289	4.38	150,567	4.55	157,086	4.22	177,506	3.96	199,811	4.04
National Debt	67,252	2.63	114,589	3.76	44,967	1.36	13,008	0.35	45,498	1.01	115,250	2.33
Other (incl. Reserves)	76,481	2.99	102,371	3.36	76,422	2.31	41,230	1.11	74,902	1.67	99,378	2.01

Sources: For 1962 and 1963 amounts taken and percentages calculated from data in Bureau of Statistics, Office of the Prime Minister, *Japan Statistical Yearbook, 1965* (1966), p. 476-481; and for 1964-1967 from *Japan Statistical Yearbook, 1967* (1968), p. 472-47c.

Table VIII – A PRIMARY FORECAST OF GROSS NATIONAL EXPENDITURE, 1968-1975

Calendar Year	Total GNP[1] Billions of Dollars	Personal Consumption %[2]	Gross Private Domestic Investment %[2]	Government Purchases %[2]	Net Exports %
1968	141.9	52.1	38.7	9.0	0.2
1969	164.8	51.6	39.1	9.0	0.4
1970	191.3	51.0	39.4	9.0	0.6
1971	222.1	50.4	39.8	9.0	0.8
1972	257.9	49.9	40.2	9.0	0.9
1973	299.4	49.3	40.6	9.0	1.1
1974	347.6	48.7	41.0	9.0	1.3
1975	403.5	48.1	41.3	9.0	1.5

[1] From Table I and II above.

[2] Calculated on basis of average annual per cent change as given in Table VI.

Table IX – A COMPARISON OF INDICES OF CONSUMER PRICES AND WAGES, 1960-1968
(Base year: 1965)

Year	Index of Consumer Prices	Index of Average Monthly Wages of Regular Workers	Index of Average Daily Wages of Casual and Day Workers in Establishments Employing	
			30 plus persons	5-29 persons
1960	74.0	61.1	58.4	48.6
1961	77.9	68.0	66.7	60.0
1962	83.2	75.0	74.1	69.6
1963	89.5	83.0	79.5	70.4
1964	92.9	91.3	95.2	83.6
1965	100.0	100.0	100.0	100.0
1966	105.1	110.8	108.9	124.0
1967	109.2	124.2	125.3	139.3
1968	115.0	141.8	142.9	137.8
Average annual increase, 1960-1967:	5.0%	9.0%	9.6%	13.0%

Sources: Calculated from data in Bureau of Statistics, Office of the Prime Minister, *Monthly Statistics of Japan*, No. 93, March 1969, p. 80, 82, 86.

Table X – INDEX OF PRODUCTIVITY OF NON-AGRICULTURAL LABOR, 1960-1967
(Base year: 1965)

Year	Index of Employed Persons in Non-Agricultural Labor[1]	Index of Industrial Production[2]	Index of Productivity[3]
1960	85.4	58.0	67.9
1961	88.1	69.2	78.5
1962	90.8	74.7	82.3
1963	93.8	83.2	88.7
1964	96.7	96.3	99.6
1965	100.0	100.0	100.0
1966	103.9	113.1	108.8
1967	112.2	134.8	120.1
Average annual increase:	3.8%	11.0%	7.5%

Sources: [1] Calculated from data in Bureau of Statistics, Office of the Prime Minister, *Monthly Statistics of Japan*, No. 93, March 1969, p. 8.

[2] *Ibid.*, p. 17.

[3] Index of production divided by index of employment.

Regardless of the merits of the argument, labor's demand for stepping up the rate of wage increases seems bound to be effective, largely because of the growing manpower shortage. Whereas in 1955, 70.8% of the population fifteen years of age and older were participating in the labor force, in 1960 that percentage had dropped to 69.2%, and in 1965 to 65.7%.[3] One major explanation is that the primary pool from which management was accustomed to recruit its blue collar workers, the new 15-year-old graduates of the nation's middle schools, is drying up. Traditional respect for education and growing affluence are inclining more and more of these youngsters to seek higher education. Whereas 46.3% of them entered the labor force in 1950, the percentage dropped to 42.6% in 1955, 28.6% in 1960, and 24.5% in 1965.[4] In absolute terms, the number of new middle school graduates available for jobs in 1965 was one-third less than in 1950, and all indications are that the trend will continue. The result is that the Japanese labor force is not only increasing in age and therefore rigidity, but also is declining in size relative to the total population. The competition of the market, therefore, will reinforce labor's demands, with the result that the present allocation of national resources will be under pressure from two directions; first, from labor, to step up the proportionate allocation for wages, and second, from management, to step up the allocation for research and development in an effort to offset the rising cost of labor by improving its productivity.

BRIDGING THE TECHNOLOGICAL GAP

Thus, the demand for higher wages can be expected to feed a second demand for a greater allocation of resources for research and development to bridge the technological

[3]Bureau of Statistics, Office of the Prime Minister, *Japan Statistical Yearbook*, 1967, p. 544.

[4]Calculated from data *ibid.*, p. 55.

gap. Business has never ploughed as large a proportion of its resources into research and development as have firms in other advanced countries. The government likewise has kept down its expenditures for science and technology. In 1963-64, for example, Japan devoted only 1.3% of its GNP for this purpose, placing it seventh in the world, in which the U.S.A. ranked number one with 3.4%. Instead of devoting large resources of its own to the development of new technology, Japanese enterprises by and large have found it more efficient to leave advanced research and development work to others, preferring to await the results, import the tested models and pay the royalties for subsequent production in Japan. Accordingly, the percentage of GNP devoted to research and development expenses (1.3-1.4%) and the percentage of the national budget devoted to science and technology (3.2-3.3%) have remained rather stationary over the past five years.

But the cream has now been skimmed and Japan faces the prospect itself of having to help fill the saucer. With Japanese industry becoming so strongly competitive in the world market and the Japanese market itself becoming so attractive to foreign firms, the cost of importing foreign technology has been going up.[5] Foreign firms have become more and more cautious about licensing the use of their technology without limiting the market it may be used in or without insisting on their own capital participation in joint ventures. Moreover, the technology which Japan is increasingly interested in, such as that related to nuclear energy, aeronautics, electronics, space, and the like, is more and more derived from the vast "big science" complex of joint government and private effort, whose transfer is not only very costly, but also frequently complicated by its relevance to advanced and highly sensitive military uses. These trends, plus the growing shortage of labor and the rising sense of nationalism, have been bringing many

---

[5]Science and Technology Agency, *White Paper on Science and Technology, 1968* (1969), pp. 5-16.

Table XI – AN INTERNATIONAL COMPARISON OF PER CENT OF GNP
ALLOCATED TO SCIENCE AND TECHNOLOGY, ABOUT 1963

Country	Year	Per Cent of GNP[1]
U.S.A.	1963/64	3.4
U.S.S.R.	1963	2.7
U.K.	1964/65	2.3
Netherlands	1964	1.9
France	1963	1.6
West Germany	1964	1.4
Japan	1963	1.3

[1] OECD Survey (1967) as cited in Science and Technology Agency, *Summary, White Paper of Science and Technology, 1967* (1968), p. 28.

Table XII – RESOURCES ALLOCATED TO RESEARCH AND DEVELOPMENT, 1959-1968

Year	Per cent of GNP spent for Research and Development[1]	Per cent of National Budget spent for Science and Technology[2]
1959	1.11%	2.73
1960	1.15	2.91
1961	1.27	2.50
1962	1.33	2.54
1963	1.30	2.80
1964	1.34	3.25
1965	1.36	3.22
1966	1.33	3.23
1967	1.41	3.22
1968	N.A.	3.30

Sources: [1] Science and Technology Agency, *White Paper on Science and Technology, 1968* (in Japanese, 1969), p. 58.

[2] For 1964-1968, *ibid.*, p. 122; and for 1959-1963, calculated from science and technology expenditures *ibid.*, p. 122, and total expenditures on the General Account in Bureau of Statistics, Office of the Prime Minister, *Japan Statistical Yearbook, 1967*, p. 470. The figure for 1968 is based on the original budget.

businessmen, as well as scientists and some officials, to demand a heavier allocation of both private and public resources to research and development. But how much more of the GNP should be allocated to this purpose? At a cost to what? And who should take the responsibility, government, private enterprise, or both?

PUBLIC IMPROVEMENTS

A third demand will be for greater allocations for public improvements. One reason will be to improve the level of living of the urban population, which, as one of the unplanned side effects of Japan's extraordinarily rapid growth, has been growing at a virtually unmanageable rate. As recently as 1955 only 45.5% of the Japanese people were living in cities with a population of 50,000 or more. By 1965 the proportion had risen to 58.2%. If the trend continues at the same rate (1.27% a year)—and there is no indication that it will not—that proportion will reach 70.9% by 1975. In a short twenty year period, Japan's cities will be burdened with more than 37 million people they did not have before. One can easily imagine the magnitude of the problem involved in trying to devise an environment capable of meeting the minimum needs of these migrants, as well as the more established residents, for such things as housing, sanitation, transportation, and the like, let alone their desires for a humane and pleasant community with good schools, recreation facilities, and cultural opportunities. The fact is, these needs and desires are not being met. Like the weather, urban conditions are more complained about than changed. But certainly in the 1970s as conditions worsen, demands for such vital public improvements will be heightened. These demands of the general public will be supported and partly shaped also by business, which faces serious problems of finding suitable locations for its continued expansion, and requires a nationwide improvement of communication and transportation facilities. They will be accompanied also by demands from

Table XIII – GROWTH IN URBAN POPULATION, 1955-1975

Year	Total Population (A) (1,000)	Population Residing in Centers of 50,000 or More (B) (1,000)	(B)/(A) (%)
1955	89,276	40,657	45.5
1960	93,419	48,526	51.9
1965	98,275	57,185	58.2
		– Primary Forecast –	
1970	103,744	67,019	64.6
1975	109,925	77,937	70.9

Sources: For 1955 to 1965, data taken or calculated from Bureau of Statistics, Office of the Prime Minister, *Japan Statistical Yearbook, 1967* (1968), p. 19. For 1970 to 1975, total population estimates from Table IV above, and other data calculated on basis of average annual percentage increase in final column for period from 1955 to 1965 (1.27%).

those who remain in rural areas, which, being drained of much of their most vigorous population, face a growing inability to support the public services and improvements they require.

THE DEMANDS OF THE FARMERS

The rural population, in addition, can be expected to press hard for a fourth demand, increasing allocations to equalize the incomes of the rural and urban population. Japan faces here the classic problem of all rapidly industrializing societies. The small private entrepreneur usually needs capital—and in the case of the Japanese farmer, land as well, since the size of his plot has been legally restricted. As a result, although he has greatly improved his productivity over the years, he has not been able to raise it anywhere near the level of the industrial worker. Moreover, to the extent that he does increase his productivity, he tends to force a decline in the prices for his output since the domestic market for agricultural products, rice in particular, is not very elastic.

In the face of this dilemma, the Japanese farmer has taken a variety of remedial measures. For one thing, farmers have moved to the cities in increasing numbers. As Table XIII implies, the percentage of the population residing in centers of less than 50,000 persons, commonly referred to as rural, has been declining steadily from 54.5% in 1955 to 41.8% in 1965. If this continues at the same rate, the rural population may be expected to fall to 29.1% in 1975. This means a drop in absolute numbers from 48.6 million people in 1955 to 41.1 million in 1965 and to a projected 32.0 million in 1975. Second, those families who have preferred to remain in rural areas have been taking on other occupations, the great majority of them sending their most active members into the cities to supplement the family income by urban commercial or industrial employment. Accordingly, the number of persons employed in agriculture and forestry has declined even more sharply,

68   *James William Morley*

Table XIV – INDEX OF PRODUCTIVITY OF AGRICULTURAL, FORESTRY,
AND FISHERY LABOR, 1958-1967
(Base year: 1965)

Year	Index of Employment	Index of Production	Index of Productivity
1958	125.4	84.7	67.5
1959	120.6	87.7	72.7
1960	119.6	90.8	75.9
1961	116.3	94.2	81.0
1962	113.0	97.3	86.1
1963	106.9	95.6	89.4
1964	103.2	98.5	95.4
1965	100.0	100.0	100.0
1966	96.8	103.0	106.4
1967	84.7	110.6	130.6
Annual average increase, 1958-1967:			7.0

Sources: Index of Employment derived from data in Bureau of Statistics, Office of the Prime Minister, *Monthly Statistics of Japan, March 1969,* p.8.

Index of Production *ibid.,* p. 14.

Index of Productivity equals index of production divided by index of employment.

Table XV – A COMPARISON OF PRODUCTIVITY OF AGRICULTURAL, FORESTRY AND FISHERY LABOR WITH THAT OF NON-AGRICULTURAL LABOR, 1958-1967

Year	Non-Agricultural Industries			Agricultural, Forestry and Fishery Industries			Comparison
	(A) Employment (1,000 persons)	(B) Production (Bil. yen)	(C) Productivity (1,000 yen)	(D) Employment (1,000 persons)	(E) Production (Bil. yen)	(F) Productivity (E/D) (1,000 yen)	(F/C) (%)
1958	28,050	7,674.2	274	15,200	1,670.6	110	40
1959	29,060	8,607.1	296	14,620	1,739.0	119	40
1960	30,090	10,667.9	355	14,490	1,884.3	130	37
1961	31,050	12,778.2	412	14,090	2,132.0	147	36
1962	31,020	14,634.2	457	13,690	2,278.0	166	36
1963	33,130	16,914.0	512	12,960	2,439.3	188	37
1964	34,170	19,559.3	572	12,510	2,559.7	205	36
1965	35,320	21,683.4	614	12,120	2,900.6	239	39
1966	36,710	25,009.2	681	11,730	3,288.6	280	41
1967	39,670	29,517.1	745	10,270	3,975.0	387	52

Sources: Employment data in Bureau of Statistics, Office of the Prime Minister, *Monthly Statistics of Japan, March 1968,* p. 8

Production data *ibid.* p. 118.

from 37.2% of the labor force in 1955 to 22.5% in 1965.[6]
At this pace, it will drop to only 7.5% in 1975, or little
more than 4 million persons. Third, those persons continuing to farm have tried to increase their productivity by
more advanced technology. Fourth, they have made heavy
and effective demands on the government artifically to
support the prices of agricultural products and otherwise to
subsidize modernization of agriculture.

The government has responded with a number of aids.
Since the nineteenth century it has carried on an extensive
program of technological education. Recently, it has begun
to promote the formation of cooperatives in an effort to
increase farming scale. This year it has inaugurated a new
program of rice diversion payments to encourage farmers to
move land out of rice, which currently occupies about 40%
of the planted area, and into other crops for which demand
is higher. But the government's primary response has been
rice supports. Domestically it has built a food control
system under which the government buys up the entire
crop of rice and a substantial portion of the wheat and
barley crops at highly inflated prices and resells what it can
at reduced prices. What it cannot sell, it stores. Internation-
ally, it carefully restricts what it feels are competitive
foreign imports by an elaborate system of tariffs, quotas,
and instruments of state trading.

For the immediate objective, equalizing rural and urban
incomes, these combined actions by the rural families themselves and by the government have been remarkably successful, in fact, more than successful. After long years of
inequality, in 1967 for the first time the average annual
income of farming households was raised to a point
actually higher than that of the urban wage earners.[7] But
the allocation of resources to achieve this goal has been
under growing attack. After all, the direct cost to the
national budget is mounting alarmingly. Calculated as a

---

[6]Ministry of Agriculture and Forestry, *Agricultural White Paper, 1968.*
[7]Ibid.

proportion of the GNP, the deficit in the government's special account for foodstuff control has risen steadily from 0.1% in 1958, for example, to 1.2% in 1967 (See Table XVI). If it continues to rise at this rate, it might reach 1.6% in 1970, and 2.2% in 1975, or $8.8 billion (3,196.8 billion yen)—presumably a fifth or more as large as the national budget! In addition, there are the indirect costs of inflation borne by the entire population. Rice prices have been pushed up from 1958 to 1967 at the rate of 6.7% a year and the average price of all agricultural products, at the rate of 6.6%.[8] These in turn have been a major ingredient in the mix that has produced an annual increase in the general average of all consumer prices at the annual rate of 5.0%. These domestic criticisms are reinforced by complaints from foreign agricultural producers, who would like to expand their sales in the Japanese market and feel sure that they could if the import barriers were lowered. With balance of payments problems becoming more and more serious for some of Japan's most important trading partners, particularly the United States, these foreign pressures too are bound to intensify.

If the present rapid urban shift of population continues and agricultural productivity continues to rise, one can foresee that the relative plight of the farmer should have been eased by the mid or late 1970s, so that the dismantling of the protective system should then be politically much easier. But pressure for change is already high both from Japan's own urban population and from the foreign powers to begin the dismantling process now, allowing food prices more nearly to find their own levels in the free market, reallocating some of the resources formerly used to protect this sector to other purposes, stimulating the farmers to speed up their exodus to the cities, and for those who remain on the land, pushing them faster into larger scale, more scientific, and more diversified

[8]Bureau of Statistics, Office of the Prime Minister, *Monthly Statistics of Japan 1968* (1969), pp. 82, 85.

Table XVI – GOVERNMENT EXPENDITURES FOR FOODSTUFF CONTROL, 1958-1975

Year	Receipts (Bil. yen)	Expenditures (Bil. yen)	Balance (Bil. yen)	Balance (Bil. dollars)	Deficit as % of GNP
1958	538.7	532.5	+6.2	+0.02	–
1959	555.9	573.3	-17.4	-0.05	0.1
1960	579.9	612.2	-32.3	-0.08	0.2
1961	626.7	629.1	-2.4	-0.01	0.0
1962	672.9	726.7	-53.8	-0.15	0.3
1963	764.5	771.3	-6.8	-0.02	0.0
1964	791.1	929.1	-138.0	-0.38	0.5
1965	908.9	1,069.9	-161.0	-0.45	0.6
1966	964.0	1,225.5	-261.5	-0.73	0.7
1967	1,030.6	1,554.2	-523.6	-1.46	1.2
Average annual increase, 1958-1967:					0.12
– A Primary Forecast – (Based on a projection of the average increase in annual share of GNP, 1958-1967)					
1970			1,101.6	-3.06	1.6
1975			3,196.8	-8.88	2.2

Sources: Bureau of Statistics, Office of the Prime Minister, *Monthly Statistics of Japan, March 1969*, p. 115.
% of GNP is calculated on the basis of GNP data in Tables I and II above.

operations. But this is strong medicine indeed. The cry of rage from those deprived would be raised in every village throughout the land. The decision this year to hold the line on the producers' price for rice has already had that effect! Compensating supports equally costly and equally frustrating to real reform might well be demanded. A change in policy will surely come, but it will take a shrewd political leadership indeed to decide when, at what pace, and at what cost.

INCREASING SOCIAL SECURITY

A fifth demand will be for expanded social security benefits for the entire nation. Traditionally, of course, the individual looked to his family to protect him from the vicissitudes of personal misfortune and social change; but, under the political pressure of shifting values, the dislocations of rapid growth, and foreign example, over the past twenty years Japan has built a social security structure which confers benefits similar to those of most advanced nations in the world. These include medical, unemployment, and accident insurance; annuities for old age, total disability, and survivors; relief for minimal living, education, housing, medical and other costs; welfare care for mothers, children, the aged, and victims of accidents; public health services; and such related benefits as pensions, assistance to war victims, and special countermeasures related to housing and employment. Already in 1965 expenditures for health alone were absorbing 3.7% of the nation's GNP, and those for all forms of social security, including health, 5.0%. The share of the costs borne by the government accounted for 21.4% of the national budget.

The total is low in comparison with other advanced non-Communist countries. In 1962-63, for example, Japan ranked eighth among such countries, both in the proportion of its GNP devoted to social security and in the absolute amount spent for this purpose per capita. The per capita amount for Japan was estimated that year at about $36

Table XVII – EXPENDITURES FOR HEALTH AND WELFARE, 1957-1975

Year	Expenditures for Health		Expenditures for Social Security*		Government Share as % National Budget
	Amount in billions of yen	As % of GNP	Amount in billions of yen	As % of GNP	
1957	324.3	2.9	456.2	4.1	
1958	353.1	3.1	504.3	4.5	
1959	389.9	3.0	579.0	4.5	
1960	442.6	2.9	657.4	4.2	
1961	546.2	2.9	788.9	4.1	
1962	651.1	2.6	921.3	3.7	19.27
1963	796.6	3.3	1,123.3	4.6	19.29
1964	989.5	3.4	1,347.5	4.7	20.16
1965	1,173.7	3.7	1,603.7	5.0	21.42
1966	1,300.2	3.6	1,867.0	5.1	20.38
Average annual increase:		0.08		0.11	
Primary Forecast, 1967-1975 (Based on annual average increase, 1957-1966)					
1967	1,592.4	3.7	2,238.0	5.2	
1970	2,685.9	3.9	3,787.7	5.5	
1975	6,246.6	4.3	8,861.5	6.1	

*Expenditures for Social Security include expenditures for all items mentioned in the text, including Health.

Sources: For 1957-1966, expenditures from Welfare Ministry, *Welfare White Paper, 1968* (in Japanese, 1968) pp. 450-451; and % of GNP calculated on basis of GNP figures at current prices for 1957-1958 in Bureau of Statistics, Office of the Prime Minister, *Japan Statistical Yearbook, 1967* (1968), pp. 503; for 1959-1967 in Table I above, and for 1970 and 1975 in Table II above. Figures for percentage of national budget allocated to governmental expenditures for social security represent the sum of percentages for "Social Security" and "Pensions" in *Japan Statistical Yearbook, 1965* (1966), pp. 476-481, and *Japan Statistical Yearbook, 1967* (1968), pp. 472-474.

(13.845 yen) as compared with $281 (101,010 yen) spent by the first ranking country, Sweden.[9] This reflects the fact that the system in Japan is new, the amount of each of the benefits is relatively small, and the public is only slowly becoming accustomed to relying on them. But the trend is clear. In view of foreign experience, the rapid rise in certain costs such as those of medicines and medical care and the prospect of continuing changes in society and social values, one must assume that costs will continue to rise and pressure for expanded services will intensify. The experience of the past ten years supports this. From a GNP allocation of 4.1% for all social security purposes in 1957, the proportion had risen by 1966 to 5.0%. If this rate of growth continues, it can be expected to result in a demand on the GNP of 6.1% in 1975. The question for the 1970s therefore is how much more of the national resources to allocate to social security. The pattern has been to hold public expenditures fairly steady at about 20% of the national budget, pushing an increasing burden on the individual citizen. But how long can this go on? How much of any expansion should be paid for by the public, and how much by the private sector? What competing purposes are to be sacrificed?

IMPROVING THE EDUCATIONAL SYSTEM

A sixth demand will be for an improved system of higher education. The avidity of Japanese children and their parents for education beyond the present compulsory level of 9 years (through middle school) has already been noted. If one may assume—as seems reasonable—that the proportion of children of the appropriate 15 to 17-year-old age group who attend high school will continue to increase at the same rate as in the recent past (2.4% annually from

[9]International Labor Organization, *The Cost of Social Security* (1967), cited in Yano Tsuneta Kinenkai, comp., *Nihon Kokusai zue* (The state of Japan in charts and tables) (1968), p. 494.

1960 to 1965), onc may forccast that whereas that proportion stood in 1960, for example, at 59.4%, and in 1965 at
71.5%, it will rise in 1970 to 83.6%, and in 1975 to 95.7%
(See Table XVIII). This, however, should not place any
new, serious demand on the total allocation of the nation's
resources for high school education, for, even so, the
number of students in high school can be expected to
decline. This is the result of the baby boom in 1947-49 and
the decline in birthrate in the years that followed. The
number of children in that age bracket, which peaked at
about 7 million in 1965, is now in steady decline. It will
probably bottom out in 1974 at about four and one-half
million. The issue of resources for this educational level will
be, therefore, not how much larger a share of the GNP
should be allocated, but rather what percentage of the costs
should be borne by the public, and what percentage by the
private, individual. This will become particularly acute if—as
seems quite likely—high school attendance is made
compulsory, for about one-third of Japan's high school
education is now being given in private institutions.

At first glance, the financial issues posed by education at
the junior college and four-year-college level may appear
similar to those of the high school level, since the peak
enrollments also will have passed by the 1970s. Like the
15-17 year-olds, the 18-31 year-old age group also
increasingly wants more education. The result is that the
proportion of those of appropriate ages attending either
junior colleges or four-year colleges has been rising steadily
from 9.6% in 1960, for example, to 14.5% in 1965. Projected at the same rate, it will reach 20.4% in 1970, and
24.3% in 1975. On the other hand, the absolute size of the
population affected by these percentages, like that of the
younger group, also reflects the impact of the baby boom.
This group peaked in 1968 at about 9.4 million. Its decline
can now be expected to continue through 1975, when it
may number about 6.5 million. The conflicting impact of
the rising demand for higher education and the declining
size of the age group makes 1969 probably the peak year

for junior college and four-year college enrollments, with approximately 1,680,000 students. Hereafter, the number will gradually decline through 1975, when it may drop to 1,574,000, a level slightly less than that of 1968.

The problems which will plague the junior colleges and universities in the 1970s, therefore, are not those of providing more spaces for an expanding enrollment, but rather of equalizing the opportunity for higher education and improving its quality. The question of equality is raised by the fact that national and other publicly supported institutions have not kept pace with the expansion in educational demand. The result is that more and more of the students have been forced to seek education in private institutions (71.4% in 1966), which are extremely weak financially and are therefore forced to charge increasingly higher fees than institutions which are publicly supported. Academic charges per student at a private university in 1955, for example, were 1.7 times higher than for a student at a national university. In 1966 they had risen to 2.5 times as much (See Table XIX). They would, in fact, have had to go up to nearly four times as much to cover the rising costs, but the steepness of such a rise is beyond public tolerance as parental complaints and particularly student protest clearly shows. The stop-gap solution has been borrowing by the universities. By 1965, loans had reached a level roughly equivalent to all personnel costs.

With no outlook for being able to service such a growing debt except by attempting further tuition hikes or further loans, the private university authorities and the parents are inevitably turning to the government for relief. The government, of course, has been helping private institutions on a modest scale, but what is now being demanded is massive. Grants are being requested to reduce and eventually abolish the private university's dependence on excessive tuition (that is, tuition in excess of the national university average) and borrowing. It is difficult to estimate just how much money may be involved, but very rough calculations suggest

Table XVIII – CHANGES IN ENROLLMENTS IN HIGHER EDUCATION, 1960-1975

HIGH SCHOOLS				JUNIOR AND FOUR-YEAR COLLEGES				GRADUATE SCHOOLS			
Year	Age Group (A) (1,000)	Enrolled (B) (1,000)	Per cent (B/A)	Year	Age Group (A) (1,000)	Enrolled (B) (1,000)	Per cent (B/A)	Year	Age Group (A) (1,000)	Enrolled (B) (1,000)	Per cent (B/A)
1960	5,452	3,239	59.4	1960	7,114	682.0	9.6	1960	8,355	15.7	0.2
_1965_	7,100	_5,074_	71.5	1965	7,195	1,041.0	14.5	1965	8,939	28.5	0.3
-Primary Forecast-				-Primary Forecast-				-Primary Forecast-			
				_1969_	9,125	_1,679.0_	18.4				
1970	5,189	4,338	83.6	1970	8,626	1673.4	19.4	1970	9,569	32.3	0.4
								_1974_	10,993	_52.8_	0.48
1975	4,705	4,502.7	95.7	1975	6,476	1,573.7	24.3	1975	10,315	51.6	0.5

Sources: For age group, Institute of Population Problems, Ministry of Health and Welfare; for enrollments, Bureau of Statistics, Office of the Prime Minister, *Japan Statistical Yearbook, 1967* (1968), p. 532, 537. Primary Forecast in each case is based on projection of average annual change in per cent of age group enrolled, 1960-1965. Underlining indicates year of peak enrollment during entire period.

that about 2.1% of the national budget, or 0.25% of the GNP, may be demanded as a new allocation for higher education in addition to that already made.

It should be remembered, moreover, that while such a new allocation would tend to strengthen the financial structure of private universities and equalize costs of higher education to students and parents, it would not solve the other important problem—upgrading the quality of the education offered. The truth is that nearly all institutions, both public and private, are in trouble. The students, who, together with the professors, have borne the brunt of these inadequacies, are now revolting—on a scale and with an intensity unparalleled among the advanced nations of the world. Nearly one-fifth of the four-year colleges and universities are now troubled by student disorder. The causes are to be found partly in the universities themselves—in their inefficient administrative structures, the isolation of much of their learning from contemporary society, the insufficiency of instructional and research salaries and facilities, and the lack of provision for the students' social environment; and partly in the larger society, where youth particularly feels the strains and frustrations produced by the war, the occupation, and the subsequent economic growth. Youth's problems will be discussed in more detail later. The point to be made here is that, while a fundamental solution of the university problem will require a complex human effort, which is now underway, very little can be accomplished without the allocation of a much larger proportion of the nation's resources than in the past. An increase in faculty and research salaries across the board will be required, as well as an improvement in academic equipment and student social facilities which could easily raise the demand for a supplementary allocation to 3 or 4 per cent of the national budget or to something like 0.5% of GNP. The pressure will be on in the 1970s to bring about this reallocation.

The pressure will also be on for strengthening and enlarging the research institutes and graduate schools.

Table XIX – DEPENDENCY OF PRIVATE UNIVERSITIES ON EXCESSIVE TUITION AND BORROWING, 1955-1966

Tuition & other Academic Fees in excess of those charged at National Universities

Year	Excess charged per student		(C) Total increase (Mil. yen) (A x B)	(D) Borrowing (Mil. yen)	(C + D) (Mil. yen)	Total (E) % National Budget	(F) % GNP
	(A) Students	(B) Yen / As % of charges at national universities					
1955	312,364 (59.7%)*	17,744 / 70%	5,386.4				
1965	660,899 (70.5%)*	56,860 / 130	38,911.9	40,932.4	79,844.3	2.1	0.25
1966	745,154 (71.4%)*	71,700 / 150	53,427.5				

Note: *Percent of total university students, including those at national and other public universities.

Sources: (A) Ministry of Education, *Wagakuni no shiritsu gakko 1967* (Our private schools) (an Educational White Paper, 1968), p. 242.
(B) Drived from data, *ibid.*, p. 154-155.
(D) *Ibid.*, p. 250.
(E) Based on National Budget data in Table VII above.
(F) Based on GNP data in Table I above.

These, particularly the latter, have not played as major a role in Japanese education as in the West, but interest in this area is now growing. Whereas there were only 15,700 Japanese students working for advanced degrees in 1960, there were 28,500 in 1965. If one projects the same average rate of growth into the immediate future, there will be some 38,300 in 1970, and 51,600 in 1975, more than three times as many as in 1960. It is not now clear to what extent private enterprise will provide the advanced training, research, and development it requires; but whether private enterprise expands its activities or the government supports an expansion of the graduate schools, there can be no doubt that for education at this level, as at the under-graduate level, pressure will increase in the 1970s for a greater share of the GNP.

MILITARY STRENGTH

There is a seventh area in which there has been consid-erable speculation abroad. That is the military. Over the years Japan has been steadily increasing the size of its annual military expenditures, from $0.4 billion (160 billion yen) in 1960, for example, to $1.3 billion (483.8 billion yen) in 1969. These allocations are enabling it to build a strength which, by the conclusion of the Third Defense Build-Up Program in 1971, will include a Self-Defense Force approximately of 180,000 uniformed personnel, organized into thirteen divisions and equipped with medium tanks, artillery, and HAWK surface-to-air missiles; a Mari-time Self-Defense Force of approximately 142,000 tons, including destroyers, submarines, and anti-submarine air-craft; and an Air Self-Defense Force of approximately 880 aircraft, centering on F104J and F-4E Phantom inter-ceptors, NIKE-AJAX surface-to-air missiles, and the BADGE Automatic Radar (warning and control) system. This is clearly a force of limited range and depth, but it is modern and reasonably well designed for its purpose of defending the home islands against a conventional attack for that short period until America's more massive power can be brought into play under the Mutual Security Pact.

But there can be no doubt that Japan will want to strengthen its military force in the years to come, for the desire for greater self-reliance in military matters continues to grow. A basic issue of the 1970s, therefore, will be: how much military build-up and for what purpose? The hawks would like to increase the percentage of GNP devoted to military force, the highest target figure responsibly discussed being 1.5% by 1975. By international standards this proportion would still be small, far below most other countries in the world. However, given the assumed growth of Japan's GNP discussed above, it would probably mean nearly a five-fold increase in annual defense expenditures in only 6 years, from $1.3 billion (483.8 billion yen) this year to $6.1 billion (2,179.1 billion yen) in 1975 (See the Maximum Alternative Forecast in Table XXI)! This would presumably suffice to provide Japan with a much more sophisticated arsenal of modern weapons for regional as well as home defense, but probably not a nuclear capacity, even if one were desired. But there is now no deep sense of threat in the country. It must be assumed that the real defense of Okinawa, after it is returned, will continue to be provided by the United States as long as it maintains substantial bases there. Consequently, once the current fever subsides to try to appease a supposed American desire that Japan expand its military efforts as a *quid pro quo* for the return of the administration of Okinawa, it is difficult to imagine the crisis, short of a clear threat of attack or the withdrawal of American protection, which would enable the government to change the pace so drastically.

There are those, of course, who take a much more limited position, arguing that defense expenditures should be expanded only to the level permitted by the established trend in the GNP share, which on the average has been declining at the rate of 0.2% each year over the past ten years. If this trend continues in the years immediately ahead, the proportion in 1975 will have dropped to 0.72%.

Table XX — AN INTERNATIONAL COMPARISON OF DEFENSE EXPENDITURES, 1967-1968

Country	Defense Expenditures		Per Capita Defense Expenditures		Defense Expenditures as per cent of GNP
	Bil. dollars	Bil. yen	Dollars	Yen	
1. U.S.A.	73.0	26,280.0	367	131,982	9.8
2. U.S.S.R.	34.5	12,402.0	146	52,653	9.6
3. China	6.9	2,484.0	10	3,450	9.2
4. France	5.5	1,980.7	110	39,701	5.3
5. West Germany	5.4	1,928.9	93	33,430	4.3
6. U.K.	5.3	1,922.4	97	36,733	5.7
7. Italy	1.9	680.4	36	13,001	2.9
8. Poland	1.7	598.3	52	18,730	5.4
9. Canada	1.6	564.8	77	27,631	2.7
10. Czechoslovakia	1.5	522.7	102	36,540	5.7
11. India	1.4	492.5	3	964	3.3
12. Australia	1.3	460.1	109	39,154	4.9
13. Japan	1.1	387.0	11	3,873	0.90 (FY 1967 (settled budget)
	1.2	422.1	12	4,175	0.83 (FY 1968 initial budget)
	1.4	483.8	13	4,786	0.84 (FY 1969 initial budget)

Source: *Kokubo* (National defense), August 1969, p. 289.

Given the probable rate of increase of GNP, this course is doubly attractive. It would still permit an increase in the absolute amount allocated—by 1975 about $2.9 billion (1,045.9 billion yen), or nearly twice as much as in 1969, while at the same time freeing an increasing portion of the GNP for other needs.

But this is not likely to satisfy the demand for greater self-reliance, so that a middle position between these two extremes may gain widest acceptance; that is, a decision to try to hold the line on the share of the GNP now being so allocated, possibly somewhere around the 0.9% average of the past five years. This would in fact represent a reversal of the declining trend of the last decade. It would nearly triple the annual expenditure by 1975, raising it to $3.6 billion (1,307.4 billion yen). This in turn would permit a substantial strengthening of Japanese defense capabilities in the adjacent sea lanes and air space.

FOREIGN AID

Finally, there will also be pressure for increased foreign aid. It should be recognized at the outset that Japan's response to the demands for aid of the developing countries, particularly in Southeast Asia, has been increasing. In the ten years from 1959 to 1968 it has increased its contribution more than 5 times, raising the absolute amount from $190.2 million (68,472 million yen) to $1049.3 million (377,748 million yen). In so doing it has now joined the big four in this field, its aid in absolute amount ranking fourth among the non-Communist nations after the U.S.A., West Germany and France.

The government is committed to aid, partly as an instrument indirectly to feed Japanese business, partly as an instrument of foreign influence, and partly as a prestige symbol among the advanced nations of the world. However, aid is hardly popular at home. One alternative policy for the early 1970s would be, therefore, to try to hold the share of GNP allocated for this purpose to a fairly fixed

Table XXI – PROPORTION OF GNP SPENT FOR DEFENSE, 1960-1975

Year	Defense Related Expenditures		Defense Expenditures as Per Cent. of GNP %
	Bil. dollars	Bil. yen	
1960	0.4	160.0	1.00
1961	0.5	183.5	0.95
1962	0.6	213.8	1.01
1963	0.7	247.5	1.00
1964	0.8	280.8	0.98
1965	0.8	305.4	0.97
1966	1.0	345.1	0.94
1967	1.1	387.0	0.90
1968	1.2	422.1	0.83
1969	1.3	483.8	0.84
Average annual decrease, 1960-1969:			0.02
— A Primary Forecast[1] —			
1970	1.6	564.7	0.82
1975	2.9	1,045.9	0.72
— An Alternative Forecast[2] —			
1970	1.7	619.8	0.9
1975	3.6	1,307.4	0.9
— A Maximum Alternative Forecast[3] —			
1970	2.1	757.5	1.1
1975	6.1	2,179.1	1.5

[1] Based on a projection of the average annual decrease in share of GNP, 1960-1969.
[2] Based on a projection of the average annual share of GNP, 1959-1969.
[3] Based on a projection of the average annual increase in share of GNP needed to attain 1.5% in 1975.
Forecasts for 1970-1975 are calculated on the basis of GNP data in Table II above.

Table XXII — FOREIGN AID, 1959-1975

| Year | Total Amount | | Per cent of GNP |
	Mil. dollars	Mil. yen	
1959	(190.2)*	68,472	0.53
1960	246.1	88,596	0.46
1961	381.4	137,304	0.46
1962	286.2	103,032	0.49
1963	267.7	96,372	0.39
1964	291.0	104,760	0.36
1965	485.8	174,888	0.55
1966	625.1**	225,036	0.62
1967	797.5**	287,100	0.67
1968	1,049.3	377,748	0.74
Average annual increase, 1959-1968:			0.023

— A Primary Forecast —
(Based on a projection of the average annual
increase of share of GNP, 1959-1968)

Year	Mil. dollars	Mil. yen	Per cent of GNP
1969	1,253.3	451,188	0.76
1970	1,511.3	544,068	0.79
1975	3,631.5	1,307,340	0.90

— An Alternative Forecast —
(Based on a projection of the per cent of GNP allocated in 1968)

Year	Mil. dollars	Mil. yen	Per cent of GNP
1969	1,219.5	439,020	0.74
1970	1,415.6	509,616	0.74
1975	2,985.9	1,075,124	0.74

*DAC Secretariat estimates.

**Provisional figures.

Sources:　Calculated on basis of GNC figures in Tables I and II above, and total official and private net contributions, 1957-1968, in OECD, Development Assistance Committee, Annual Aid Review (1969). *Report by the Secretariat and Questions on the Development Assistance Efforts and Policies of Japan* (mimeo, 1969), Table 1.

Table XXIII – AN INTERNATIONAL COMPARISON OF FOREIGN AID PROGRAMS
OF DAC MEMBERS, 1968

Country	Total Amount (Mil. dollars)	Rank	Per cent of GNP	Rank
U.S.A.	5,676	1	0.65	12
West Germany	1,635	2	1.24	3
France	1,483	3	1.24	3
Japan	1,049	4	0.74	7
U.K.	845	5	0.73	8
Italy	493	6	0.68	9
Canada	308	7	0.49	16
Netherlands	276	8	1.10	6
Belgium	243	9	1.15	5
Switzerland	242	10	1.43	2
Australia	187	11	0.68	9
Sweden	129	12	0.50	15
Austria	74	13	0.66	11
Denmark	74	13	0.55	14
Portugal	74	13	1.45	12
Norway	58	16	0.65	12
TOTAL	12,845		0.77	

Source: OECD, *Annual Aid Review 1969: Summary of 1968 Flows* (1969), Table
4.

level, say, for example, the 0.74% of 1968, allowing the
absolute amount to grow precisely in accordance with the
growth of the Japanese economy. This would in fact result
in nearly tripling the amount by 1975! Government spokesmen, however, have publicly pledged their support for the
goal called for by the LDC's, 1 per cent of GNP, and
pressure is building to move toward that goal. The question

is: at what pace and at the expense of what other purposes? The least disruptive pace would probably be to
continue to increase the proportion of GNP allocated for
this purpose at the same average annual rate of increase
sustained in the past decade (0.023%) (See Table XVII).
This would result in 0.90% of GNP by 1975, when the
absolute amount might reach $3,631.5 million (1,307,340
million yen)—or more than three times that in 1968, and
point to a closing of the gap to 1% of GNP by 1980.

THE PROBLEM OF CHOOSING

Each one of these eight demands, as well as others not
mentioned here, has its own justification. While each would
undoubtedly command wide support if it could be met
without reference to the others, this is impossible, for each
represents a claim on the nation's resources which, if met,
would affect both the overall growth rate and the amount
left for the satisfaction of the others. Complex judgments
will be required on the rightful priority of each in the
context of the whole. The basic question of the 1970s,
therefore, will be whether the Japanese will be satisfied to
continue straining almost singlemindedly to sustain and
possibly increase their rate of economic growth, assuaging
unwanted side-effects with stop-gap measures and deferring
other desires to a later time; whether they will demand the
purpose of growth be more directly sought, even if it
means slowing the pace. In this case, what is the purpose
that will win support? Is it, for example, to build the
instruments of international power and seek thereby the
foreign influence and prestige they have so long been
denied? Or is it rather to equalize the opportunities at
home and raise the level of living for all to the point which
the few have already attained?

No one can doubt that once the Japanese people have
made up their minds, they will move dramatically. However, the possibility of reaching such a decision in the early
1970s seems at the moment remote. This is a society that

works by consensus, and there is no clear consensus yet. Moreover, the political forces required to produce such a consensus are in disarray.

The vast social and economic changes already referred to have inevitably been eroding the power base of several of the established political parties. The urban migration especially has weakened the Liberal-Democratic Party, which was built on a coalition of farmers and businessmen. In the move to the cities, many of its former supporters have given up their old allegiance. Some to find a new home with one of the other parties, but most, it would seem, float among them according to the mood at election time. Even those back in the villages are growing restless, particularly the young, over concern that the LDP may be softening its support for rice price supports. Among urban workers, the steady improvement of wages has similarly weakened their allegiance to the Socialist Party, which has depended so heavily on organized labor, particularly the unions of the majority labor federation, Sohyo, for support. The individual working man has grown increasingly pragmatic in his affluence. He is less and less inclined to follow the strident, ideological pleas of the Socialist Party, and more and more inclined, like the new city dweller from the country, to float about among the other opposition parties, looking for a new home that he has not yet found.

At the same time, while the old actors are changing roles, two new actors are entering the scene. One is youth, a strata which was indulged, but little listened to, in the recent past. It now promises to play a much larger role in the politics of Japan as in most other societies. In statistical terms, its core may perhaps be identified as primarily the age group from about 18 to 26, a period in Japanese life when the individual is least disciplined by responsibility. Generally speaking, it is then that he leaves home, usually for the first time, to go to college or to find work in the city. Usually unmarried, he lives with his peers the single, barracks-like life of the student in cheap lodgings or the employee in company dormitories. He knows that later he will be expected to marry, settle down, and conform—and this, generally speaking, he himself expects to do; but, for the first time he feels relatively free, and in the exuberance of his energy and his idealism, and often in the depth of his loneliness and frustration, he is inclined to thrash out at the established order and demand change. All political parties have felt his revolutionary impact. None has been able to represent or to manage him.

Similarly, at the other end of the age spectrum, another group is now emerging: the retired, the people who have retired from their usual employment generally at about the age of 65. Thanks to improving health standards, while they can expect to live another decade or more, the breakdown of the traditional family system leaves them to face that decade with special apprehensions. They are developing their own life style, living alone in apartments, no longer with family responsibilities, but with problems of employment, housing, social security, and cultural participation, which are relatively unique for Japanese society and which do not have a really adequate champion in the parties as now constituted.

The impact of these social movements has steadily eroded support for the ruling conservatives. From a high of 74.5% of the seats in the House of Representatives in 1949 and 66.1% of the popular vote in the general election of 1952, they have declined steadily, losing popular votes at about the average rate of 1.15% a year, finally in 1967 slipping below the half-way mark to 48.8%. Skillful management of the electoral system enabled them even in that year to hold on to 57% of the House seats; but, if the slippage in popular support continues at the same rate, it will be 44.2% in 1971, by which time the next general election will have to have been held, and 39.6% in 1975. Were this to happen, the Liberal-Democrats would almost inevitably lose their control of the House and their ability to form a government. If they cannot check the slippage, they will clearly enter a time of crisis following the next election. In this situation, some leaders will step up their efforts to replace the past leadership and policies in order to try to check the decline. Others can be expected to step up their negotiations with the other parties and factions to explore the possibility of uniting the LDP with one or more of them in a coalition government, or splitting from the LDP and forming with them a new party to take over. These maneuvers will likely be facilitated by the splitting or transfer of allegiance of various of the conservative factions as Premier Sato and about half of the other current faction leaders (six of the present 12 are already over 65) begin to move off the scene. Thus, it seems clear that the 1970s—probably the early 1970s—will be a time of political change in Japan, with interest groups re-forming in order to channel the new pressures described above, and with the political parties re-grouping in an effort to find a new format, both of organization and of policy, which will appeal to a stable voter base.

Out of this scramble, a younger and bolder leadership with a clear vision of the future may succeed in building a new political machine, seizing power, and heading the nation on a decisive new course, but the odds are against it. Age and experience will still be respected, and such men are perplexed by the issues. Consensus will still be sought, and such consensus is impeded by increasingly heated political maneuvering. No doubt high economic growth will continue to be attractive, and modest bows will be made to each of the special demands that are insistently presented, but none will be fully satisfied. In short, the early 1970s will likely be a time not of decision, but of temporizing. Until the issue of political leadership is settled, the fundamental question on the nation's agenda: growth for what? will have to wait.

JAPAN'S GROWTH AND JAPANESE-AMERICAN RELATIONS

The significance of this analysis for Japanese-American relations would seem to be the following:

1. Although the expanding GNP and heightening confidence of the Japanese people make it almost certain that, in absolute terms, Japan will continue to enlarge its trade, its aid, and its military establishment, thereby playing a larger and larger role in the world, it is unlikely, at least by the early 1970s, to opt clearly to reduce its concentration on economic growth and begin a serious new drive for international influence. This suggests that no dramatic shift in the direction or character of its foreign relations is in prospect.

2. In the bilateral relationship between the United States and Japan, which can only grow more important to the two countries as the years go by, the problems of trade, investment, and security which require negotiation are inextricably bound up with complex, unresolved domestic problems. Until decisions are made in the domestic field—which seems unlikely in any decisive way by the early 1970s—these bilateral foreign problems cannot be fully resolved. We can expect in the early 1970s to move closer to the goal of a more equal, more mutual, more completely satisfying relationship, but not fully to attain it.

3. But the domestic problems which challenge the Japanese people today and will continue to do so in the 1970s—the overall problem of priorities and the specific problems of industrial structure, agricultural adjustment, education, city life and the like, should be recognized not simply as impediments to the resolution of certain bilateral difficulties, but also as new opportunities for helping each other and strengthening the sense of community between us. After all, we in America face many of these problems, not in the same, but in similar guise. We, too, seek ways to improve the workers' lot, keep down prices, ease the farmers' problems, enlarge social security rebuild our cities. improve our schools, advance our science, and still play a constructive and peaceful role in the world. We need all the knowledge, experience, and vision available. So, I suspect, does Japan. Is it not time, then, that, while we continue to offer each other so much in other ways, we consider in the

1970s much more seriously than we have in the past how to expand, through seminars, conferences, internships, and joint research projects, the interchange of our ideas and our experience on these social problems?

4. Japanese Economic Cooperation in Asia in the 1970s

SABURO OKITA

FOUR STAGES IN JAPAN'S ECONOMIC COOPERATION

The course of Japanese economic cooperation since World War II can be divided into the following four approximate stages.

The first stage opened with the start of reparation payments. The first reparation agreement, concluded with Burma in 1954, was followed by similar agreements with the Philippines, Indonesia, and the Republic of Vietnam. Economic assistance to Laos, Cambodia, and the Republic of Korea during this period actually was a form of reparations. Because the funds under these agreements were intended as compensation for wartime damages, the Japanese government did not seek to exert any control over their use or any voice in evaluating their contribution to the economic development of the countries concerned. Recently it has become common practice for donor nations to review recipient states' utilization of economic aid to insure effective use of the funds, but under these reparation and semi-reparation agreements such procedures were necessarily ignored.

The second stage was marked by economic cooperation in the form of loans and investments. A loan to India in 1958 was the first of this type. Arrangements during this stage covered both exports and imports, including deferred payment for Japan's exports of plants and machinery as

Table I. Reparations and their Fulfillment
(in millions of dollars)

	Amount Promised	Status of Payments (Dec. 1968)	Fulfillment Percentage (Dec. 1968)	Period of Payments
Burma	200	200	100%	April 1955 - April 1965
Philippines	550	314.8	57.1	July 1956 - July 1975
Indonesia	223.3	212.9	95.3	April 1958 - April 1970
Vietnam	39	39	100	January 1960 - January 1965
Total	1,012.3	766.7	75.7	

Source: *Main Statistics Concerning Economic Cooperation;* Ministry of Foreign Affairs; May, 1969

well as various forms of financing for development, and imports to secure a supply of raw materials and resources. The major concern during this period was to meet the needs of Japanese industry, and little consideration was given regional priorities in loan and investment policies. Investments were made, for example, in the Minas steel mill in Brazil, pulp plants in Alaska, and oil exploitation in the Middle East. The commercial aspect of this Japanese aid raised problems from the beginning, but in view of the fact that Japan's per capita national income at the time (1958) was $284, a level common among aid recipient countries in 1970, it was perhaps inevitable that contribution to the Japanese economy was emphasized.

Japan entered its third stage around 1965-66, when economic aid became an integral part of Japan's overall Asian policy. It was in this stage, marked by the emergence of a conscious attempt to give regional priority to East and Southeast Asia, that Japan concluded agreements for economic cooperation with Taiwan and South Korea, became an active participant in establishing the Asian Development Bank, and took the initiative in convoking the Southeast

Table II.   Total Japanese Aid and Aid to Asia (excluding Middle East)
(in millions of dollars)

	Total Aid	Aid to Asia	Government-Based Aid	Government-Based Aid to Asia
1959	196		97	70
1960	224	140	87	82
1961	377	162	107	93
1962	297	149	87	86
1963	320	179	140	116
1964	361	248	116	116
1965	601	321	244	205
1966	669	385	285	216
1967	855	500	391	343
1968	1,049	559	357	311
Total	4,573	2,644	1,911	1,643

Source *Main Statistics Concerning Economic Cooperation;* Ministry of Foreign Affairs; May, 1969

Asia Ministerial Conference for Economic Development.
Japanese moves in assistance since the spring of 1969
may indicate the beginning of a fourth stage. At the Fourth
Southeast Asian Ministerial Conference for Economic
Development held in Bangkok in early April, Foreign
Minister Aichi, linking the United Nations Second Development Decade with the proposed plans for a Decade of
Peace and Development in Southeast Asia, stated that "the
Japanese GNP might well reach the level of $500 billion by
1980, and the magnitude of economic cooperation which
will then be extended by Japan will exceed levels we can
now conceive of." About a week later at the Second
Meeting of the Board of Directors of the Asian Development Bank in Sydney, Australia, Finance Minister Fukuda
delivered a speech in which he said, "It is my desire to
double the flow of our aid to the Asian region within the
coming five years." Mr. Kiuchi, representing Japan at the

Table III. Japanese Aid to major Asian Nations
1959 - 1968
(in millions of dollars)

	Total Aid	Government-Based Aid
Republic of Korea	442	180
China (Taiwan)	183	64
Burma	180	161
Philippines	470	256
Indonesia	451	388
Thailand	160	27
South Vietnam	44	44
India	483	330
Pakistan	144	151
Ceylon	25	15
Total (including) other Asian areas)	2,644	1,643

Source: *Main Statistics Concerning Economic Cooperation;*
Ministry of Foreign Affairs; May, 1969

Table IV. Aid by DAC Nations to Less-Developed Countries
(in millions of dollars)

	1966	1967	1968	1968% of GNP
Australia	148	192	187	0.67
Austria	49	48	74	0.66
Belgium	178	164	243	1.15
Canada	267	254	306	0.49
Denmark	21	25	74	0.55
France	1,320	1,341	1,483	1.24
Germany	728	1,140	1,635	1.24
Italy	632	287	505	0.70
Japan	625	798	1,049	0.74
Netherlands	254	228	276	1.10
Norway	17	30	58	0.65
Portugal	40	78	(74)	1.45
Sweden	108	121	127	0.49
Switzerland	110	134	(242)	1.43
U. K.	939	841	845	0.83
U.S.A.	5,020	5,565	5,676	0.65
DAC Total	10,464	11,247	12,855	0.77

Source: *Development Assistance;* OECD Development Assistance Committee; 1968

25th ECAFE General Assembly held in Singapore soon after the Sydney meeting, also referred to the Decade of Peace and Development in Southeast Asia and touched upon the possibility of doubling Japan's aid. These and other similar statements leave the strong impression that Japan has begun to accept a positive commitment to economic cooperation in Asia. It is reported that agreement was reached in the Cabinet Ministers' Meeting for Economic Cooperation held on July 11 to approve as Government policies Foreign Minister Aichi's idea for "Economic Development for Southeast Asia in the 1970's" and Finance Minister Fukuda's idea of "Doubling Aid to Asia in Five Years."

Table V. Japanese Trade with Asia (see Table VI)
(in millions of dollars)

	Exports		Imports	
	Amount	% of Total	Amount	% of Total
1954	703	23.2	575	23.9
1955	727	36.2	663	26.8
1956	868	34.7	734	22.7
1957	969	33.9	789	18.4
1958	876	30.4	591	19.5
1959	988	28.6	759	21.1
1960	1,307	32.2	915	20.4
1961	1,384	32.6	975	16.8
1962	1,465	29.7	967	17.1
1963	1,608	29.3	1,211	18.0
1964	1,782	26.7	1,293	16.3
1965	2,195	25.8	1,406	17.2
1966	2,630	26.9	1,613	16.9
1967	2,931	28.1	1,795	15.4
1968	3,613	27.8	1,984	15.3

Source: *Twenty-Year History of Postwar Japanese Trade;* Ministry of International Trade and *Industry (MITI); 1967: and 1969 MITI White Paper.*

Until recently, Japan has been somewhat negative about
liberalizing the terms or increasing the volume of its aid,
usually citing for justification Japan's low *per capita*
national income or the instability of Japan's international
balance of payments. The apparent shift towards a more
positive commitment to Asian economic development is
probably the consequence of its achieving in 1968 a GNP
surpassed only by the United States and the Soviet Union
and a very favorable balance of payments, both of which
contribute to a new sense of global responsibility. This
positive approach may also be a reflection of such economic and political developments as the planned withdrawal of British troops from the area east of the Suez, the
expected withdrawal of United States forces from Vietnam,
the Nixon government's so-called "partial disengagement
policy" in Asia, Japan-U.S. negotiations over the reversion
of Okinawa, and the expiration of the original ten-year
term of the U.S.-Japan Security Pact in June of 1970.

Japanese Trade and Southeast Asian Development[1]

Japan resumed diplomatic relations in 1952 with the
coming into effect of the San Francisco Peace Treaty. By
1955 Japanese government and business circles were
speaking of Southeast Asian development. At that time, the
concept of "combining American capital with Japanese
technology for the development of Southeast Asia" was a
popular one. However, this idea never materialized, due in
part to the rather unsympathetic reception given it by
Southeast Asian nations.

Japanese industry around 1955 regarded Southeast Asia
as a crucial export market and as a source of natural
resources needed by Japanese industry. Roughly 40% of
Japan's exports were going to Southeast Asia, and there

---

[1]For the purposes of this paper, the region referred to as Southeast Asia
includes South Korea, the Ryukyu Islands, Taiwan, Cambodia, South Vietnam,
Thailand, Malaysia, Singapore, the Philippines, Indonesia, Burma, India,
Pakistan, Ceylon, and Afghanistan.

Table VI. Japanese Trade with Asia
(in millions of dollars)

	Exports from Japan			Imports to Japan		
	1958	1963	1968	1958	1963	1968
Rep. of Korea	56.7	159.7	602.7	11.0	26.9	101.6
Ryukyu Islands	65.4	135.5	266.1	14.9	64.5	87.9
Hong Kong	100.1	246.4	467.6	10.6	28.8	54.0
Taiwan	90.0	107.1	471.6	75.6	122.6	150.7
Cambodia	8.4	14.5	20.3	1.4	3.9	6.6
South Vietnam	39.5	33.3	198.9	1.3	6.0	2.7
Thailand	83.8	181.0	365.4	21.7	90.7	147.0
Malaysia	14.3	56.2	104.5	159.3	269.9	343.4
Singapore	77.2	111.9	209.2	12.7	22.4	61.8
Philippines	89.5	150.3	411.1	99.8	230.2	397.9
Indonesia	49.0	49.1	146.6	37.0	104.8	251.8
Burma	41.4	76.3	39.3	12.3	20.1	12.4
India	84.8	153.7	139.3	74.4	125.6	293.0
Pakistan	22.0	47.8	116.0	34.2	47.7	56.9
Ceylon	34.6	21.9	24.6	7.3	9.6	12.3
Afghanistan	9.2	9.1	13.1	0.3	0.1	0.0

Source: *1969 MITI White Paper.*

was little hope for any significant increase in trade with mainland China because of the international political situation. It was in this stage that the "rice bank" concept, the concept of increasing food production in some Southeast Asian countries for export to Japan, and other such ideas were widely discussed.

Enthusiasm for Southeast Asian trade, however, diminished during the subsequent ten year period from 1955 to 1965. Trade among the advanced nations of the world showed a dramatic increase during this period, and Japanese trade with North America, Europe, and Australia increased

Table VII. Japanese Trade with Communist Asia
(in millions of dollars)

	Exports			Imports		
	1958	1963	1968	1958	1963	1968
China	50.6	62.4	325.4	54.4	74.6	224.2
North Korea	–	5.3	20.7	0.0	9.4	34.0
North Vietnam	1.4	4.3	2.4	6.9	10.3	6.1
Mongolia	–	0.5	0.4	0.0	0.1	0.6

Source: 1960, 1964, and 1967 *MITI White Papers.*

Table VIII. Japanese Trade with China
(in millions of dollars)

	Exports	Imports
1954	19.1	40.8
1955	28.5	80.8
1956	67.3	83.6
1957	60.5	80.5
1958	50.6	54.4
1959	3.6	18.9
1960	2.7	20.7
1961	16.6	30.9
1962	38.5	46.0
1963	62.4	74.6
1964	152.7	157.8
1965	245.0	224.7
1966	315.2	306.2
1967	288.3	269.4
1968	325.4	224.2

Source: 1960, 1964, and 1969 *MITI White Papers*.

at a much greater rate than with the less developed nations, including those in Southeast Asia.

Southeast Asia's share of total Japanese exports, which exceeded 40% until approximately 1954, fell to 26% by 1966. This is partly attributable to Japan's preoccupation with acquiring advanced-nation standing as symbolized by OECD membership and IMF Article 8 status, the world-wide decline of the relative share of trade with the less-developed nations, and the lack of awareness in Japan of the complex realities of local Southeast Asian political and economic conditions during this period.

The revival of interest since 1965 in Southeast Asian development is due to a number of factors. One economic factor is that the Southeast Asian share of Japanese trade began to show a modest upward trend. Furthermore there were signs of an emerging new pattern of trade with the nations of the region. For example, the rapid industrialization of South Korea, Taiwan, and Hong Kong, particularly their development of light industries, stimulated exports to high-income markets, including Japan. As a result, it was expected that Japan's trade with the region would shift from a simple vertical pattern of trade relations (raw materials in exchange for finished goods) to a horizontal pattern) in which various manufactured goods are ex-changed. Such expectations stimulated various kinds of Japanese private investment and joint ventures in the region. Another factor in this general revival of interest in Southeast Asia is the Japanese government's new attitude, mentioned above, that aid policies are to be regarded as an integral part of its overall Asian policy.

The implications of these recent developments for future trade relations between Japan and the states of Southeast Asia are far reaching. For some time to come, Southeast Asia will continue to be an important source of raw materials and agricultural products which Japan will seek in increasing quantities as its economy continues to grow at a rapid pace. Conversely, Japan will become an increasingly important market for Southeast Asian exports. During the

1960-65 five-year period the ECAFE developing nations increased their exports to Japan by 82% while their overall trade expansion was only 23%.

Southeast Asian countries have begun to show a heightened enthusiasm for economic development and a more pragmatic approach to aid problems. Fears of economic imperialism and opposition to foreign private investment have given way somewhat to a greater willingness to welcome foreign technology, management, and capital to stimulate economic development.

Sixty percent of Japan's total raw material imports now 60% come from advanced nations. Her rapidly expanding economy has forced her to seek raw materials not only from Southeast Asia but from North America, Latin America, Africa, Australia and Siberia as well. But since Japan's raw material requirements are expected to continue to rise, there is still considerable room for Japan to increase its imports of raw materials and agricultural products from the less-developed countries.

The problem of the local processing of these raw materials will become increasingly important because of the general reluctance among the less-developed countries to export raw materials, such as lumber and metal ores for example, in unprocessed form. Japan will probably try to meet this problem by extending financial, technological, and managerial cooperation to these nations and accepting raw materials for import in processed or semi-fabricated form. In effect, the rapid growth of the Japanese economy and the resultant demand for increased imports will continue to function as an important stimulus for the economic development of Southeast Asia and particularly its resource industries—mining, forestry, fishing and agriculture.

The Impact of Increased Wages and Labor Shortages in Japan

Japanese wage increases and labor shortages are having an important effect on the economies of Southeast Asia. This effect, first felt in Hong Kong, Taiwan, and South Korea, is expected to reach Thailand and Singapore in the near future and India, Indonesia, and Pakistan eventually.

Industrial wages in Japan rose by an average of 14% in 1968, and at the present rate of increase are expected to double in five years. Since Japanese wages are already three to four times those in South Korea and Taiwan, and since South Korean and Taiwanese wages are more than twice those of Indonesia, Japanese industry no longer has the advantage it enjoyed when Japanese labor was abundant and cheap. Other Asian nations are likely to be in an increasingly advantageous position to compete with Japanese industry.

Having already become a net importer of silk in 1966, Japan similarly became a net importer of cotton yarns in 1967. Exports of cotton textiles are declining by roughly 10% every year. At the same time, the exports of other Asian nations are increasing, indicating that these countries have developed competitive power vis-a-vis Japan in such fields as rubber products, toys, artificial flowers, footwear batteries, low cost transistor radios, and so forth. The same is also true of agricultural and marine products.

It is against such a background that the traditional Japanese industries employing large numbers of workers are facing competition from other Asian nations in United States, Canadian, Australian and European markets. In this competition Japanese exports have been suffering a relative decline while other Asian nations have been strengthening their position.

There has also been a noticeable flow of the products of these industries from other Asian nations into the Japanese domestic market. Embroidery and artificial flowers from Hong Kong are typical examples, but there are indications that the impact is not limited to light industry alone but will be felt in heavy industry as well. For example, South Korea and Taiwan are reported to be capable of producing cast iron products at one-third of Japanese cost, and there is every reason to expect that some of the parts for machinery, automobiles, electronics, and other industries will in the future be produced in such Asian countries for export to Japan.

Therefore one can argue that Japanese wage increases and labor shortages have stimulated the industrialization and increased the exports of such neighboring nations as Hong Kong, Taiwan, and South Korea, and that these exports have in turn been an important factor in the high growth rates recently achieved by these economies. While it is true that special procurements for the Vietnam war in the last several years have also contributed to the high growth rates of the economies of states in the Vietnam area, it is also true that the Japanese wage increases and labor shortages are another, long-term cause of that economic expansion. To cite the South Korean example, the 1968 real growth rate of 13.3% (as against a nominal growth rate of 26.8%) was the second highest in its history, surpassed only by the 13.4% achieved for 1966, and raised the *per capita* national income to $139.00.

In a fashion somewhat similar to the historic effect that the British industrial revolution of the 19th century had on the European continent and later on North America, Russia, Japan, and elsewhere, the sustained growth of the Japanese economy with its consequent import expansion, wage increases, and labor shortages is stimulating economic growth and export expansion in other Asian nations at a steadily accelerating tempo and in an ever greater variety of ways. Recently the Indian government has also begun considering the possibility that many Indian industries will be made competitive by Japanese wage increases and labor shortages, with the result that trade in mutually complementary industrial products may be developed between the two nations. In fact, at the beginning of this year, the Japanese sewing machine industry placed an order to India for some of its cast iron parts.

Agriculture, Industry, and Aid in Southeast Asia
As noted above, Japan's economic growth, both directly and indirectly, stimulates an increased rate of economic

growth and trade for other Asian nations. This Japanese contribution is made primarily by private business. Particularly worthy of note are the joint ventures established in Hong Kong, Taiwan, and South Korea, as well as licensing arrangements between Japanese firms and firms in these countries, for providing Japanese technological know-how. The local industries chosen for such arrangements have generally been those which seemed likely to yield favorable results in lower production costs and greater export competitiveness. These arrangements also promote local private enterprise, and these countries' ties with Japan have often resulted in their developing new export products.

Another point to be borne in mind in this respect is that the Japanese economy was at a level similar to the current level of the other Asian economies not very long ago, and its own experience provides a useful example for these countries in dealing with such basic problems as labor surplus and capital shortage.

In agriculture, "miracle rice" has come to be widely cultivated in Asia and, as the phrase "the green revolution" suggests, production of rice, wheat, and corn is rapidly increasing in the region. Particularly in the case of rice, labor-intensive cultivation, the use of high-yield strains, irrigation, fertilizers, insecticides, and other such techniques were generally developed in Japan, Taiwan, and South Korea. This Japanese-type labor-intensive cultivation has been applied to good effect in the region, along with the results of research and development by international organizations. In some cases, Japanese experts have provided direct technical assistance and training, while in other cases experts from abroad have learned Japanese techniques and then worked to implement them. At any rate, it is fair to say that Japanese experience and technology, both industrial and agricultural, are playing a vital role in accelerating the economic development of other Asian nations.

However, since Japan now suffers from a rice surplus, there is little hope that the once cherished concept of increasing Southeast Asian rice production for import to

Japan can be realized. While the high production costs of rice in Japan make the plan still theoretically feasible, the Japanese domestic political situation makes it very unlikely that large quantities of rice will be imported in the foreseeable future.

On the other hand, there is still considerable room for Japanese imports of such animal feed grains as maize and sorgum, and soy beans or other agricultural products which are produced in Japan in only limited quantities. Some of these grains are already being imported from Southeast Asia. Maize imports from Thailand are one recent example. Thai exports, which stood around 30 thousand tons ten years ago, have now increased to nearly one million tons, most of which are earmarked for Japan. It is expected that this same pattern will also prevail in future trade with Indonesia, Cambodia, and some other countries of the region.

Moreover, increased production of foodstuffs in Southeast Asian nations results in a saving of foreign currency which until now has been spent for food imports, and thus serves to strengthen these countries' purchasing power. In turn, this savings improves the chance of increased imports from Japan and other industrial nations.

However, a major problem in food production, particularly rice, is how to manage the economies of such major rice exporting nations as Thailand and Burma and Vietnam, too, when the situation there stabilizes, so as to cope effectively with rice surpluses which may develop in the future. The strong influence that the regional supply of and demand for rice will have upon the future of the Thai economy was one of the reasons prompting Thailand to propose at the Fourth Southeast Asian Ministerial Conference for Economic Development that a study for Southeast Asia of the major economic problems in the 1970's be made under the auspices of the Asian Development Bank. Another reason was concern for the impact which the withdrawal of British troops and settlement of the Vietnam war will have upon the international balance of payments of nations in the region.

If these eventualities are to be met, it is essential that agricultural production be diversified and industries developed which can, in part, be turned to exports. In this respect Japan can play an increasingly important role.

Future Developments and Japanese Policy

As the scale of aid to and trade with Southeast Asia increases, Japan's economic relations with the area will become all the more important. Japan's share of the Philippine import market, for example, increased from 13% in 1957 to 30% in 1967. A tentative Japan Economic Research Center projection of the Japanese economy for 1975 indicates that Japan's share of total Southeast Asian imports may increase from 1965's 17% to 35% by 1975. Regardless of their preferences, trade with Japan is expected to be vitally important to Southeast Asian economies.

Already the Japanese GNP far surpasses the combined GNP of the developing states in the ECAFE region stretching from Pakistan and India to Indonesia, South Korea, and Taiwan. It is inevitable that the future course of the Japanese economy will influence the economies of these nations. In turn, this makes it necessary that Japanese domestic policies be considered in the wider perspective of their impact upon the economies of the region. It was once said that "if the American economy catches cold the Japanese economy will come down with pneumonia," but it may well happen that even a slight change in the Japanese economy or trade policies could shock the other economies of the region.

For example, policies of rice loans to South Korea and Okinawa or food aid to Indonesia, natural domestic policies to deal with the Japanese rice surplus, might well create difficulties for such rice-exporting nations as Thailand and Burma. The demand by Southeast Asian nations for liberalization of Japanese agricultural and marine imports is another case in point. The balance of trade with most of these nations has been in Japan's favor for some time, and these nations are concerned with the way their economies seem to be becoming increasingly dependent upon a single country. This is certainly a legitimate concern for any nation.

Japan ought, therefore, not only to increase its imports from these countries but also expand the scope of cooperation with them in their economic development. Care should also be taken to give partner nations a greater voice so as to avoid the impression that Japan is simply exploiting their resources for Japanese benefit or working for one-way sales of Japanese products. Care should also be taken to share the benefits of such cooperation with local governments and businessmen.

Table IX. Predicted 1975 Japanese Exports
(in millions of dollars)

	Exports			Japanese Share of Market	
	1965	1968	1975	1965	1975
U.S.A.	2,479	4,086	13,019	11.6%	18.0%
Canada	214	346	1,102	2.7%	4.8%
Western Europe	1,093	1,659	5,349	1.2%	2.6%
Oceania and South Africa	512	654	2,555	7.2%	16.5%
Latin America	488	742	1,834	5.0%	8.9%
Asia	2,195	3,613	9,181	17.2%	35.0%
Total (including other parts of the world)	8,452	12,972	39,000	4.5%	10.1%

Source: "Preliminary Report of Medium-Term Projection of Japanese Economy for 1975"; Japan Economic Research Center; July 15, 1969

It is important that trade policies, technical assistance programs and financial aid be closely coordinated. With a view toward securing a supply of natural resources and linking economic assistance with the expansion of trade, it is particularly important for Japan that its aid programs be implemented in such a way as to benefit the economic development of the countries of the Southeast Asian region. A deeper study of the mechanisms of economic development in each country receiving aid is indispensable. Political opposition to bilateral aid agreements may also present problems for Japan. Increased aid through multilateral channels and international organizations such as the World Bank and the Asian Development Bank is one possible solution.

Japanese aid policies are sometimes criticized for being insufficiently coordinated among the governmental ministries and agencies concerned. Japanese industries engaging in overseas activities are also said to have difficulties with Japanese government regulations. Positive encouragement for overseas investment may become necessary. The demand for capital export liberalization as the next step in Japan's overall liberalization program is likely to draw increasing attention in the near future.

On February 16, 1968, the *Keizai Doyukai* (Japan Council for Economic Development) published its "Suggestions Concerning Economic Cooperation." The report made recommendations on "Unifying Policies for Economic Cooperation," "Budgeting and Planning for Foreign Aid," "Revising the Overseas Economic Cooperation Fund Law," "Expanding Technical Cooperation and Improving Its Effectiveness," "Fundamentally Reviewing the Foreign Exchange Act and Foreign Trade Management Act," and "Concluding Investment Guarantee Agreements."

While Japan has increased the amount of its aid considerably, the criticism remains that the terms of its aid are relatively hard compared with other member countries of the Development Assistance Committee. Naturally, the terms and quantities of aid should be appropriate to the recipient nation's stage of economic growth and development and its absorptive capacity. The pattern and amount of aid should therefore differ with each recipient nation. Those nations which have made substantial progress in their economic development are increasingly capable of absorbing funds on nearly commercial terms, and are therefore most concerned with the amount of capital that can be supplied them. In contrast, those countries whose economies are still in an early stage of development and countries which are only first embarking in a major way on economic development programs are more in need of long term, soft loans.

Even within the same state, near commercial term loans may be appropriate for manufacturing industries, while grants or very soft loans are desirable for projects such as elementary education, technical training, health and sanitation and improvements in nutrition. Improvements in the agricultural infrastructure, transport facilities, communications and power may fall in between the above two categories.

In summary, Japan's future aid policies must be governed by the need to meet the particular requirements and stage of development of each recipient country in Southeast Asia. It should also emphasize cooperative arrangements with other donor nations as well as with the various international organizations engaged in economic development work.

Table X. Economic Growth Rates for East Asian Nations

	1963	1964	1965	1966	1967
Taiwan	14.2	17.3	10.5	10.9	12.9
Korea	40.6	42.7	15.3	27.7	20.0
Philippines	21.8	11.6	8.5	11.7	5.1
Thailand	5.7	7.0	10.2	19.1	9.0
South Vietnam	6.8	14.1	23.7	68.8	–

Note: Nominal GNP Growth Rates

Source: *1969 MITI White Paper on Trade.*

5. The Future of United States Policy in Southeast Asia
GEORGE McT. KAHIN

ENDING OF THE VIETNAM WAR: SOME REACTIONS AND CONSEQUENCES

The point of departure for most discussions of future American policy in Southeast Asia is the prefatory remark: "Assuming some sort of an honorable settlement in Vietnam. . ." or "on the assumption that the United States leaves Vietnam in a way which is not interpreted as a defeat. . ." This is an unrealistic foundation on which to build, and not merely because the nature of the war and of the American involvement preclude any honorable ending of it for the United States. Any realistic projection of American relations with Southeast Asia must accept the fact that its Vietnam intervention will be widely regarded as a failure. Whatever the pattern and pace of the United States' withdrawal, the ultimate reckoning by Asians will be that American military and economic power, however massively applied, could not make up for a regime's lack of broad popular support, and could not overcome indigenous revolutionaries who had secured this. Nor will the lesson be lost on Southeast Asians that American intervention in a civil war can be devastingly destructive—so great as to bring the leaders of other governments that have security pacts with the United States to question whether in their case such intervention would after all be worthwhile. Quite apart from what the American public may countenance, the

114

states of Southeast Asia are in the future likely to be more circumspect towards establishing or maintaining relationships with the United States providing for its military intervention.

It is possible that a policy of protecting a truncated South Vietnamese state with a substantial residual U.S. force may for a while longer be defended before the American public under the slogan of not abandoning Asians to communism. An administration that recalls the potency of the "loss of China" issue in the campaigns of 1950, '52, and '54, might temporarily favor this course, regarding it as useful in obviating attacks from the right, from George Wallace, or others. It must be acknowledged that a President—even an unpopular one—has great power to influence the public's perception of external realities. There is certainly presidential precedent for Mr. Nixon's finding it expedient to justify policies in terms of anti-communist cliches and stereotypes, even though these may now have become discredited among many senior government officials and among intellectuals outside of government.[1]

It is likely however, that we are moving on to a new era of American foreign policy where the long-accepted rationale of anti-communism will simply not, at least when applied to Southeast Asia, develop sufficient public support for the policies of any administration. The political landscape is different from the years when Richard Nixon campaigned for the Senate and Vice Presidency, and it is not just the Wallacites that make it so. There are new forces on the left as well, articulately critical of the intervention in Vietnam and anxious to ensure that there be no

---

[1]Although apparently most policy-makers have come to appreciate the polycentric character of world communism, there is still a gap to be closed with respect to a majority of the public. The outmoded stereotype of a monolithic communism, and the auxiliary belief that communist movements in underdeveloped countries must be subordinate to Moscow and/or Peking still have wide currency among the electorate. Despite the experience of Vietnam, this confusion is likely to persist for a number of years. Some American policy-makers will probably find it expedient to take advantage of this myth, even though by doing so they reinforce it and give it an even longer life.

even remotely comparable repetition of this experience elsewhere in Southeast Asia. However overwhelming the political reaction from the right to the new student generation's progressivism, the insistence on bringing moral and humanitarian values to bear on the conduct of foreign policy is likely to have a much greater-influence than in the recent past. Not only can this be expected to develop pressure substantial enough to increase the tempo of disengagement from Vietnam; in addition, it will probably exert a significant influence on post-Vietnam policy.

By the mid-1970s, at least, United States military intervention in Southeast Asia will probably be less likely, because even where the circumstances are basically different and the parallel only superficial, a large, politically active, and vocal generation will vigorously oppose such involvement as a repetition of the Vietnam experience. This is likely to be a powerful offset to pressures urging the Administration to intervene militarily in any Southeast Asian country—including the Philippines.[2]

In any case, the Vietnam experience should have demonstrated to Americans as well as to Southeast Asians the inability of the United States to sustain governments that lack a substantial popular base, particularly where American power confronts the mainstream of a country's nationalism. It should have shown that the ranging of American (or any foreign) power on the side of one faction in a civil war will tarnish its nationalist credentials and strengthen those of the other side. Moreover, it should have become evident that heavy American military or economic buttressing of a regime can endanger its survival by insulating it from political and economic realities and rendering it insensitive to the social forces with which it must ultimately come to terms if it is to survive.

Indeed, there is some basis for concluding that if

---

[2]There is already a clear generation gap, with respect to the Philippines, and Americans in their 20s and 30s no longer see the former colony as the special U.S. responsibility that their fathers did.

American policy in Vietnam had prevailed and the National Liberation Front had been overcome, the societies of other American supported Southeast Asian countries would have suffered. For such an outcome might well have increased the social and political irresponsibility of governments already highly dependent upon the U.S. for their security, such as those of the Philippines and Thailand. With their leaders believing they could rely on U.S. military intervention to help put down any substantial insurgent opposition, even if the popular discontent generating it was widespread, these governments might well have become more insensitive and unresponsive to the needs and demands of their people. And the more they leaned on the U.S. for succor against internal insurgents, the more their nationalist legitimacy would be undermined.

An argument increasingly used by the Johnson Administration during 1967 and 1968 to offset domestic criticism of its Vietnam policy, and still flourished by its apologists, is that the venture has at least bought time for the other states of Southeast Asia. Thanks to the American intervention in Vietnam, so the argument runs, a shield has been provided behind which they have been able to rally their forces against communism, address themselves to nation building, and work out problems among themselves so that a foundation of regional collective self-defense could be laid. According to this rationalization, as a consequence of the American stand Thailand has been enabled to reorganize and strengthen its internal security; and Indonesian generals, who might otherwise have wavered, were provided with an example which stiffened their backbone against the Indonesian Communist Party and gave them the courage to move resolutely against it.[3]

[3]Indonesia's international security and internal political situation have been little affected by American actions in Vietnam. Generals Suharto and Nasution and their colleagues needed no example of American anti-communist staunchness there to be persuaded that their own immediate and direct self interest called for prompt measures against hostile local communist power which they believed threatened them. If American actions in Vietnam did have
Continued on page 118

This is a false and misleading interpretation, a remarkable illustration of how far those seeking a publicly acceptable rationalization for a mistaken policy are prepared to distort history. It is not clear yet to what extent President Nixon today embraces this particular rationale of his predecessor's policy; but in 1967 he evidently did.[4] If this reading of the past and present forms the premises upon which the U.S. bases its policies in the 1970s, those policies are not likely to be realistic. In fact, on balance the U.S. intervention in Vietnam has had a deleterious effect on most of the rest of Southeast Asia. Directly and indirectly it has both exacerbated many existing problems in the area, and has created new ones.

Animosities among the states of continental Southeast Asia have been sharpened. This is particularly evident in the relations among the Indochinese states and between them and Thailand. Not only has Laos suffered tremendous internal political disruption as a consequence of the Vietnam war, but in addition its relations with both parts of Vietnam and with Cambodia have become much more strained. Long engrained traditional animosities between the Thai and Vietnamese have been enhanced as a result of Thailand's involvement in the war. By permitting the United States to establish air bases on its territory which have played such a major role in the bombing of both

Footnote 3 continued from page 117

any significant effect on the political struggle in Indonesia it was to enable the Indonesian Communist Party to capitalize on the broadly based Indonesian opposition to the United States' intervention in Vietnam, an opposition manifest across the whole of the country's political spectrum.

If the Indonesian military leaders had any reason at all to be grateful for the U.S. intervention in Vietnam—it was because the magnitude of that involvement precluded any gratuitous American interference in Indonesia during the time that General Suharto and his allies were consolidating their power in the struggle against Sukarno and the Communist Party—a struggle wherein for some six months (1965-6) the outcome was quite uncertain. American intervention in support of Suharto would almost certainly have turned nationalist sentiment against him and strengthened both Sukarno and the Indonesian Communist Party.

[4]See Richard M. Nixon, "Asia After Vietnam," *Foreign Affairs*, October 1967.

North and South Vietnam as well as parts of Laos, Bangkok has inevitably engendered bitterness and animosity among Vietnamese. Any normalization of Vietnamese-Thai relations after an end to the Vietnam war will be all the more difficult if American bases are maintained in Thailand; for not only Peking, but also Hanoi, (as well as any South Vietnamese government not aligned with the United States) will undoubtedly feel directly threatened by the continuation of such an American military presence there.

As a consequence of the war Cambodia's relations with its two major traditional enemies, Thailand and Vietnam, have further deteriorated. This is not merely because of the many incursions across its eastern frontier by the military forces of all Vietnamese parties, but relates more importantly to the Cambodian-Thai border. Repeated probes have been undertaken from Thai border bases into Cambodian territory by South Vietnamese soldiers recruited from the Cambodian minority in Vietnam and trained by American special forces. Following a Vietnam settlement these soldiers may be repatriated or perhaps absorbed by Thailand and integrated into its own Cambodian minority areas. But even if that can be achieved, Cambodian resentment, already aroused as a consequence of earlier subversive efforts by Bangkok and Saigon, can be expected to smoulder for some time, maintaining a barrier to cooperative action between Cambodia and its two major neighbors.

The Vietnam war has had a generally destabilizing impact on many of the frontiers of continental Southeast Asia. This is by no means confined to Vietnam's borders with Laos and Cambodia. It is also true of the Thai-Cambodian, Thai-Lao and Cambodian-Lao borders. The war has served to open up the arbitrary colonially-determined boundaries, in a sense reconstituting some of the old broad and fluid traditional frontiers. Both the actual fighting and the unusual political and economic pulls arising from the war have caused upland tribal groups, particularly in Laos and the western marches of Vietnam, to become dislodged from their old base areas so that they now move much more widely, frequently across political boundaries altering local political balances and creating new economic problems. On Thailand's western border this problem was already serious because of insurgencies by ethnic minorities in adjacent areas of Burma, often stimulated by their alliances with or supplies of arms from Kuomintang Chinese troops operating there. As a consequence of the fighting in Laos, hill-dwelling Meo and Yao tribesmen, who have been drawn into the conflict on both sides, have often been obliged to flee from their home areas, a significant number forcing their way across Thailand's northern border.

American expenditures related to the Vietnam war have resulted in a considerable additional influx of dollars to Thailand, the Philippines, and Singapore as well as to Japan, Taiwan and South Korea. But this is an artificial economic stimulus that will drop precipitately after the war with predictably unsettling effects.

At the same time some of those countries most in need of American economic assistance, Indonesia in particular, have been disadvantaged because the American war effort in Vietnam has absorbed funds which might otherwise have been available to help them meet pressing problems. Because of the almost certain continuing retrenchment in American overseas aid following the Vietnam war and the likelihood that a major part of what does go to Southeast Asia will be required for the rehabilitation of the devastation in Vietnam, it is unlikely that the level available to either Indonesia, or other Southeast Asian countries will become significantly higher.

Post War Southeast Asia

Partly because of the scale of the U.S. involvement in the Vietnam war, many observers tend to over-emphasize the importance of external forces and underestimate internal factors in determining prospects for future stability in Southeast Asia. But however the Vietnam war ends and whatever the future policies of the U.S. and other major powers in Southeast Asia, most of the area is bound to be politically unstable for several decades.

Among the Southeast Asian states themselves, traditional animosities have a powerful continuing dynamic that would remain operative whether or not there had been a Vietnamese war. These locally generated frictions are in themselves quite sufficient to develop serious threats to the region's stability. Competing claims to territory are still very much alive among these states. Moreover, most of them are beset by problems of national integration, involving persisting tensions between majority groups and often large minorities, that generate problems which often affect neighboring states.

Nearly all of the Southeast Asian states emerged only very recently from colonial straitjackets that had served to contain some of the major thrusts of their traditional foreign policies. Moreover, the boundaries imposed by the colonial powers often violated regional ethnic patterns and historically-conditioned ethnic alignments. In few parts of Southeast Asia can one say that present international borders do even rough justice to previous history or ethnic patterns.[5] Throughout the area the traditional rivalry between dominant lowland peoples and the upland minorities remains sharp, divisive, and either already seriously disruptive (as in Burma, Laos, Thailand, Cambodia, South Vietnam and West Irian), or potentially so (as in Sarawak,

---

[5]The pre-colonial frontiers of continental Southeast Asia were not surveyed geographic boundaries, but were in effect something like broad no-man's lands where spheres of influence distant from the capitals converged or overlapped. The possibilities for international friction tended to be reduced by a situation wherein frontiers were not demarcated lines, but broad peripheral territories that were either highly autonomous or virtually independent of the adjacent states. Consequently these zones often served as buffers between the states. Usually these were upland or mountainous areas inhabited by ethnic minorities which frequently pursued modes of livelihood involving periodic shifting of village locale. The imposition of colonial rule established a new kind of fixed linear boundary which usually cut quite arbitrarily through tribal groupings of these upland minority ethnic groups. This was notably the case with the frontiers between Thailand and Burma, northern Thailand and Laos, Vietnam and Laos, of Northwest Cambodia *vis-a-vis* Laos and Vietnam, as well as of the frontiers between China and Northern Vietnam, Laos, and Burma.

Sabah and Kalimantan). Because most of these minority
groups straddle international bounderies, some of these
lowland—upland conflicts cannot today be confined within
existing frontiers, and could easily exacerbate existing international tensions.

An enduring political problem general to Southeast Asia
is that of the overseas Chinese minorities. Some countries
in continental Southeast Asia have pursued policies leading
to a high degree of assimilation or at least fairly harmonious relations between the major indigenous group and
these Chinese. But particularly in most of insular and
peninsular Southeast Asia[6] tensions between the indigenous
groups and those of Chinese ancestry have been severe and
are likely to remain so. The inter-ethnic tensions in
Malaysia are, of course, the most threatening of all. There
the threat of communal strife during the coming decade
will probably remain very great. Political repression of
Malaysia's large Chinese minority is almost sure to lead to
major explosions which in the long run even police state
methods will probably not be able to contain. This is a
probability which must weigh in the assessments of all the
major powers with an interest in the area.

Undoubtedly the major force making for political instability in Southeast Asia during the next few decades will be
socio-economic. It will be less related to broad, distributive
justice than to the frustration of hopes of a substantial
educated or semi-educated minority of the population made
increasingly restive because education has so badly out-
stripped the sort of economic growth that can utilize high
school and university graduates. The number of people with
a secondary or college education unable to find employment reasonably commensurate with their level of education (and thus with their expectations) is growing rapidly
every year in all of these countries. The political malaise
stemming from this cannot easily be exaggerated. Through-

[6]By the term "insular and peninsular Southeast Asia" I mean Malaysia,
Singapore, Brunei, Indonesia and the Philippines.

out Southeast Asia this increasingly widespread frustration is becoming sharper and can be expected to develop a political thrust with which even army-dominated governments must soon try to come to terms. There is no doubt that in the mid-1969 election upset in Malaysia it was the frustration of a new generation of educated Chinese with their lack of economic opportunity that combined with the already long-existing political discrimination against the country's large Chinese minority as a whole to produce the political upsurge that cut so deeply into the parliamentary strength of the governing party. In other countries where the army is not yet the major component of government, as in Cambodia and the Philippines, the political impact of unemployed and underemployed graduates, and students alarmed over jobless prospects, is likely to become much greater during the coming years. Within the decade it is probable that this phenomenon will be a major, if not the major, factor in the politics of nearly every Southeast Asian country, with the probability of a consequent growth in their political instability.

Violent political change, sometimes revolutionary in nature, is and will for a long time remain a normal political process in Southeast Asia. Since its governments do not incorporate institutions which provide effectively for any significant measure of peaceful alteration in the socio-economic or political *status quo*, this is only likely to occur when physical power is brought to bear against *status quo* governments, either to force change or else to replace them with new regimes.

It is, after all, basically through political violence that the present socio-economic orders and patterns of ethnic relationship have been maintained in these states. In most cases the dominant political elites are unlikely to promote, or even acquiesce in, the kind of reform necessary to relieve social and economic inequities and ethnic discrimination before those who feel most aggrieved resort to violence. Because of the social pressures now building, this violence will not always be restricted to mere shifts in power within political elites and is destined to have an increasingly revolutionary character.

In countries where significant political change can come only through violence, and where reforms are badly needed, subversion of existing governments will inevitably be the principal means for accomplishing such change. But effective subversion of any of these governments can only come through indigenous forces. All variants of radical political change in Southeast Asia will inevitably carry a heavy nationalist charge. Outside intervention in these processes— whether projected from the United States, China, the USSR, or Japan—is likely to have unpredictable consequences and if at the military level almost certain to be counter-productive.

General to Southeast Asia is the danger that foreign economic aid will create artificial political situations where governments become estranged from their people and are provided with a reprieve enabling them to rule for a time without having to maintain and develop a sufficient base of popular support. Heavy reliance on outside aid, economic as well as military, even if multi-laterally channeled, can easily insulate a political leadership from local economic and political realities and reduce its sensitivity and responsiveness to socio-economic problems and political discontent.

Status quo governments cannot be expected to support social and economic changes which appear likely to weaken their power base appreciably or strengthen that of existing or potential competing political elements. Since foreign aid must be channeled primarily through existing governments, it is, of course, difficult to prevent them from using it to protect and strengthen their own power, even though this tends to increase the socio-economic inequities which provide the basis for the political appeal of dissident groups.

Undoubtedly where foreign economic assistance is provided on a multi-lateral basis it is less likely to be used primarily to maintain a regime in power, and more likely to benefit a significant part of the population, whether immediately or in the long run, by establishing some of the prerequisites for economic development. The enlightened injection of such outside economic and technical assistance can help speed needed social reforms in Southeast Asian countries. Where its application is in tune with local social and economic realities, it can sometimes temporarily reduce the likelihood of political malaise. But even where this aid is fully consonant with local development needs, and dispensed multilaterally, it may easily cause further distortion of socio-economic patterns and thereby lead to an increase rather than a reduction of the political strains within the country. This, however, is not a reason to deny such aid. For generally throughout almost the entire area any substantial amount of socio-economic change is incompatible with the maintenance of political stability. Such instability is often an inevitable transitional phase which must be gotten through before major economic and social development can occur. Indeed, the political conditions that are ultimately prerequisite for such development may sometimes be more rapidly achieved where an initial infusion of economic aid increases social strains and induces a sufficient degree of violent opposition against the government, either to displace it or force it to accept basic change.

The political stability of a recipient regime should be neither the over-all objective nor a condition for continuing foreign economic aid. Intermittent political turbulence will be for at least a generation to come a natural phase in the over-all political development of many of these countries. If outside economic assistance is to make any major contribution to their social welfare and economic growth, the donors should recognize that frequently the improved political leadership that is necessary for bringing about major economic and social progress is likely to come to power only after an intervening period of political instability.

Outside military support against political dissidence—whether it is termed "opposition" or "subversion"—is even more dangerous than outside economic support in insulating these governments from appreciating the needs of their people and responding realistically to domestic political pressures. (And the current American security relationship with both Thailand and the Philippines makes this problem something more than hypothetical.) If Southeast Asian governments are going to be viable they must be able to cope on their own with local subversion. In the long run the introduction of foreign military support cannot save them and will progressively turn the force of nationalism against them.

It is not only the introduction of foreign military forces that tends to be politically dangerous for incumbent governments in Southeast Asia; unfortunate domestic political consequences also result from supplying them with large amounts of military equipment. The more an outside power endows the leaders of one of these countries with a military capacity, the greater the likelihood that they will rely on this kind of power to resolve local problems. Their disposition to do so is increased not only by the amount of military equipment available to them; there is also a qualitative aspect that has recently become more important. This derives from the advanced level of military technology provided to these Southeast Asian governments. The sophisticated character of the military "hardware" and the techniques for its application now made available to their leaders can easily effect changes in their relationship with the people they govern. With this kind of military equipment and technology, local military establishments have the capacity to oppose political dissidence by means which permit physical distance between those applying the firepower and those they seek to control. But the more governments rely on such means of repression, the less likely it is that they will appreciate the reasons for the dissidence and the less inclined they will be to try to work out a relevant basis for political accommodation with an active opposition. And because these means of suppression discriminate so little between the actual insurgents and others who live in the area, their use is likely to be politically counter-productive.[7] They are likely either to create terror-stricken refugees (who flee to an adjacent area where they become an economic burden and cause friction with its settled population), or create local sympathy and additional adherents to the insurgent group. Use of such measures can quite easily have all of these effects.

Some Aspects of the International Context
China will always remain the major power most directly concerned with continental Southeast Asia. Her primary strategic interests require that neither the United States nor the Soviet Union become predominant in this area or draw it into an alignment directed against her. Peking will undoubtedly remain as sensitive as in the past to the threat of American bases and defense ties with Burma, Thailand, Laos or Vietnam. Soviet military ties with these states would be every bit as disturbing to her. During the 1970s China can be expected to continue to attach more importance to preventing her southern neighbors from cooperating in an American or Soviet-supported containment belt than to fomenting or supporting

---

[7]An infantry company whose objective is to maintain order in a district must interact with the local population without unnecessary provocation if it is to be effective. It can perceive the adverse local reaction to unnecessarily brutal actions, and its leaders soon appreciate that their unit's effectiveness is dependent upon the establishment of reasonably good relations with that part of the local population not actually participating in insurgent activity. Operating among them it has some capacity to discriminate between the dissident minority and the uninvolved majority. But punitive strikes by bombers, fire from helicopter gunships and artillery barrages cannot distinguish between armed insurgents and the population among whom they move. These supposed shortcuts to assertion of political control are, understandably, in the long run heavily counter-productive. This phenomenon is not peculiar to the American experience in Vietnam, but can be encountered in several other Southeast Asian countries. It has been most dramatically illustrated during the past year in northern Thailand. There strafing attacks by fighter bombers of the Thai airforce against villages, sometimes supplemented by napalm attack, have served to antagonize non-Thai tribal groups which Bangkok seeks to control, and in an overall sense have increased Thailand's now considerable problem of border insurgency.

subversive actions against their governments.[8] Particularly with the tensions on her vast Soviet frontier, it will be all the more important for China to avoid antagonizing the states on her southern border so as to induce them to accept American or Soviet military ties.

Whether or not Leonid Brezhnev's address of June 7, 1969 actually leads to some kind of Soviet-sponsored Asian security pact, Russia's involvement in Southeast Asia will apparently be greater after the Vietnam conflict is concluded than it was before. Against the background of the Soviet Union's antagonistic relationship with China and the tension over their long frontier, Moscow is likely to have an increased interest in the states which front on China's other borders. It would not be to the interests of such Southeast Asian states to be drawn into an Asian security pact directly or indirectly supported by the Soviet Union against China. Because of China's fear of hostile encirclement, they might endanger their own security at least as much by aligning with Soviet Russia as they would by continuing with or entering into military alignments with the United

---

[8]Many Western writers, including some from the Soviet Union, have recently considerably exaggerated the extent of Peking's intervention in Southeast Asia, while minimizing or disregarding that of the United States. In fact, quite apart from the case of Vietnam, the record clearly shows that U.S. political and military intervention in Southeast Asia has been far greater than Communist China's and has had a much heavier political impact—for the most part unsettling.

Vietnam is not an isolated case. It represents simply one of the most recent, and by far the heaviest and most militarized, of a series of United States interventions. Nor is this intervention in Vietnam unique in terms of futility and counter-productivity. Indeed, some of the lessons learned by the United States from its involvement in Vietnam should have been appreciated on the basis of the earlier fruitless or actually counter-productive American interventions elsewhere in Southeast Asia. But this formidable catalog of blunders has been largely unknown to Americans and to most of their representatives in Congress. Not only has the overall impact of previous United States military involvements and efforts at political subversion in many other Southeast Asian countries been a failure; in addition, the consequences of these past actions have a continuing life. In Burma, Cambodia, Indonesia and Laos one can clearly perceive today how the unfortunate political residues of American interventions during the 1950s still significantly affect the local political scene and circumscribe the possibilities for new, more enlightened, American policies.

States.

Peking's anxiety is likely to be more acute if the Soviet Union and the United States arrive at some rapprochement whereby they reach defense understandings, whether tacit or explicit, on the areas bordering southern China. If a convergence of U.S. and Soviet strategic aims towards China induced these two major powers to enter into a military pact to "contain" China, the participating states on China's southern border could easily become targets for efforts by Peking to subvert and displace their governments with less hostile political leaderships. (In such a situation, the negative nationalist reactions to the contending political groups' affiliations with major outside powers would presumably tend to cancel out.) From Peking's point of view such a "containment" role by a Southeast Asian state could not be regarded as neutral or passive and would certainly be assessed as hostile and provocative.

The magnitude of the Soviet government's support of Hanoi's war effort gives Moscow a tremendous vested interest in maintaining the cordial relationship it has developed with the North Vietnamese regime. North Vietnam is, of course, of importance to Russia not merely because of its geographical proximity to China. Although at the political-military level Hanoi may not have become a major power, because of the prestige it has won in its struggle against the United States it is likely to exert considerable ideological influence within the communist world for at least a decade. Conceivably Moscow might hope to make North Vietnam a keystone in the continental Southeast Asian sector of a Soviet-sponsored Asian cooperative security arrangement. It seems probable, however, that Hanoi would refuse any such Soviet-sponsored role, endeavoring to remain neutral in Moscow's and Peking's cold war and insisting on a position in Southeast Asia independent of both.

It is evident that Japan's future role in Southeast Asia will be a major one. Even if Tokyo's relationship to the area remains economic and does not extend to military matters, Japan will have the capacity to exercise a significant degree of influence over political developments there. I refer the reader to the papers by my Japanese colleagues in this volume for a discussion of Japan's role.

There is little to suggest that, following a Vietnam settlement, Australia can be induced again to become involved in the security of continental Southeast Asia, but the decisions taken in Canberra in mid-1969 indicate that, in company with New Zealand, Australia expects to play a significant role in insular and peninsular Southeast Asia. Although its commitment to defend Malaysia and Singapore appears to be substantially qualified and lacking in explicitness, maintenance of a small infantry force in Singapore (two battalions) together with two Australian air squadrons, and naval units, constitutes a military presence with security implications which ramify beyond Singapore and Malaysia, and which under certain conditions could at least indirectly affect defense arrangements for Indonesia and the Philippines. (In part, of course, this derives from the nature of the existing ANZUS and U.S.-Philippine security pacts.)

United States policy in the 70s

Southeast Asia is not an area of major importance to the security of the United States. It is not in the interest of the United States to enter into commitments for the defense of these countries in any way that would significantly reduce its capacity to respond to outside threats to Western Europe or Japan, both of which are much more important to American security than the whole of Southeast Asia. Moreover, the overthrow of no government in Southeast Asia would pose any real danger to American security. Irrespective of American actions, during the next decade a number of these governments will be overthrown. In some cases, their people may be better off as a consequence, although this is by no means necessarily so. With the possible exception of Laos, it is improbable that during the next decade any of the Southeast Asian governments outside of Vietnam will become communist. But, if they do, the variant of communism will almost certainly be highly nationalistic, with these states the satellites of neither Moscow nor Peking.

Certainly the United States should not abandon concern for the welfare of the area, particularly with respect to economic, educational, and technological assistance—preferably multi-laterally channelled. (And naturally with respect to the whole of Vietnam its moral obligation to provide major assistance is very great.) However, maintenance of the internal political stability of the states of Southeast Asia is not necessarily in the best interest either of the Southeast Asians concerned or of the United States. In any case there is nothing really effective that the United States can do to maintain this stability. And, efforts to provide for the international security of the states, especially those on the Asian continent, should not be undertaken by the United States unilaterally.

It has become fashionable, particularly with the advent of the new Administration in Washington, to argue in favor of the establishment of a regional Southeast Asian collective security arrangement. Although this idea was advanced during the last year or two of the Johnson Administration, it has received particular encouragement from the new Administration, with a number of writers now referring back to Richard Nixon's October 1967 article in *Foreign Affairs*. The idea of replacing an American military presence in Southeast Asia with a collective defense arrangement among non-communist Southeast Asian states undoubtedly has considerable appeal for Administration leaders and Congressmen who, while desirous of as much military disengagement from Southeast Asia as possible, do not wish to be charged with abandoning the American mission of containing Asian communism. This kind of arrangement can be presented as bespeaking a continuing responsibility toward anti-communist Southeast Asian governments, but as designed to avoid involvement of American ground forces while being much less expensive than bilateral defense arrangements between the United

States and these countries.

Those who advocate such a policy generally presuppose a continuing readiness to employ American naval and air forces as a riposte against any possible incursion by Chinese armies across Southeast Asian frontiers. It is, of course, this and the possibility of similar Soviet action which would probably constitute a major deterrent to whatever inclination Peking might have to send its armed forces into Southeast Asia. In addition, because of the failure of American ground forces in Vietnam and the history of her own relations with pre-colonial Southeast Asia, China can be presumed to have a realistic respect for the power of local nationalisms in the face of outside military intervention.

Thus, the principal objective advanced by proponents of a Southeast Asian collective defense arrangement is the suppression of insurgencies in any of the member countries—whether or not the insurgents are supported by outside communist countries. The difficulties in organizing such a system would be formidable because most of these states have supported, and will probably continue from time to time to support, subversive insurgent activities against one another. (This is true of insular and peninsular as well as continental Southest Asia.) It would not be inconceivable, however, particularly if there were the inducement of a considerable American financial contribution, for a number of these countries to join in organizing collective action against insurgent activity, whether or not it was communist in nature. Collective action by the military forces which could be contributed might be sufficient to give a beleaguered member of such a pact significant additional firepower in its efforts to suppress local insurgents. But though the host government might obtain temporary military advantage against the insurgents, nationalist sensitivities would almost certainly be aroused in a way that would further erode its base of popular support. And the social, economic and political conditions which generated the insurgency would remain. The political pressures which had been militarily contained would very likely build up to a greater intensity, later to break out with even greater force.

A common denominator among most of the more likely members of a Southeast Asian collective defense pact is antagonism towards and discrimination against their Chinese populations. Such a pact between Indonesia, Malaysia and the Philippines could conceivably bring about collective action against the Chinese minority in one of them, whether or not in the guise of "anti-subversion" or "anti-insurgent" measures.[9] If such a regional collective security arrangement postulated an American contingency backup, the United States might easily find itself in a most undesirable position.

Collective action against overseas Chinese by Southeast Asian countries would probably ruin possibilites for good relations between them and both Taiwan and Peking. Much more dangerous would be the likelihood that a regional pact that could be employed in suppressing insurgent activity by local Chinese might encourage a member government to risk increased discrimination against them. Such action would be certain to provoke reaction among the Chinese which, even though suppressed, could result in great bloodshed and tremendous economic disruption. If such a regional pack were called into operation by the Kuala Lumpur government, the consequences would almost certainly be disastrous for Malaysia, and the repercussions in member countries of the pact could be highly adverse to their interests. Unfortunately the leaders of many Southeast Asian countries have still not become disabused of their quite erroneous assumption that a corollary of the United

[9]It would seem unlikely that any Thai government would participate in collective action against overseas Chinese in any ASEAN (Association of South East Asian Nations) country. This is not only because the Thais' relationship with their own substantial Chinese minority is reasonably harmonious, but because Thailand is also the only ASEAN member situated geographically close to China. Although it is conceivable that the Indonesian government might respond to a call from Kuala Lumpur to help it maintain Malay dominance over the local Chinese, it is very unlikely that Bangkok would.

States' anti-Peking policy is antagonism towards overseas Chinese and a willingness to countenance and even encourage repressive measures against them. This is, of course, decidedly not the case. Existing American efforts to encourage the economic development of Southeast Asian countries recognize the vitally important contribution which the Chinese component of their populations has made and can continue to make.

Bilateral cooperation with Soviet Russia in maintaining the security of the states of Southeast Asia is another course about which the United States should be very circumspect. If this is essentially an anti-Chinese instrument and its overriding rationale "containment of China," the best interests of the United States are not likely to be served. Any attempt at collective security in Southeast Asia which is so oriented will probably fail in the long run and will be likely to work against rather than for the region's security. American efforts to achieve security for the area, whether or not involving cooperation with Soviet Russia, should open the door wide to full Chinese participation and keep it open, even though initially Peking is reluctant to participate.

Following a settlement with the United States, North Vietnam will not suddenly be reduced to its previous weight on the international military and political scales. It is destined to remain for some time to come by far the strongest military power in Southeast Asia, and efforts to promote the area's collective security which exclude this powerful state are not likely to be very effective. North Vietnam can make an important contribution to the security of Southeast Asia. But undoubtedly Hanoi can contribute most towards this to the extent that it is independent of both Moscow and Peking, and the United States would be mistaken to encourage it to depart from a neutral position *vis-a-vis* Sino-Russian rivalry.

The most realistic American approach to Southeast Asian security would be in terms of the area's heterogeneity, and would reflect an appreciation of the significant differences between the security problems of continental Southeast Asia and those of insular and peninsular Southeast Asia (Indonesia, the Philippines, Singapore, Brunei, and Malaysia). If China actually ever came to the point of invading a continental Southeast Asian country, logistical problems would be formidable and make the undertaking enormously expensive, though it would be possible for her to penetrate it with her land forces. (Any effort at *occupation* would, of course, be even more expensive—both financially and in terms of manpower attrition—and could probably not be effective in Burma, Thailand, or Vietnam.) Although the threat of retaliatory Soviet or American air power could well serve as a deterrent against any Chinese disposition to invade a continental Southeast Asian country by land, such action could probably not prevent an invasion if the Chinese were so oblivious to the costs and their own self interest as to undertake it. However, even if she had the disposition, China does not possess the capability to mount military incursions into Indonesia, the Philippines or even Singapore and Malaysia. The air and sea power of the United States and its Australian-New Zealand ally could easily prevent any such effort, and presumably Soviet Pacific naval and air power would be sufficient to accomplish the same.

Whether or not one regards bases in the Philippines or Singapore as important to American security, in terms of regional defenses insular and peninsular Southeast Asia should be distinguished sharply from continental Southeast Asia. U.S. security pacts with countries in the former are much less likely to be regarded as threatening or provocative by Peking than are pacts with the states of continental Southeast Asia.

It would be in the best interest of the United States to cut existing bilateral defense agreements in Southeast Asia and to eschew entering into new ones or into any entangling back-up defense commitments to a collectivity of anti-communist Southeast Asian countries. If the national self-interest of the United States so dictated, it could always intervene if invited. It does not need a military pact in advance in order to respond to a call for assistance, whether the request comes from Burma or India or Thailand or the Philippines. No longer tied to such regional military commitments, the United States would retain a greater flexibility for deploying its defensive capability in the world as a whole in conformity with its own interest as it then perceived it. Without bilateral defense agreements with the United States, the countries of Southeast Asia stand a better chance of avoiding friction with both China and with their own Southeast Asian neighbors, while the prospects for their own healthy political development would probably be improved.

Whatever course the United States follows in insular and peninsular Southeast Asia, it is essential that it disengage as soon as possible from its bilateral defense arrangements in continental Southeast Asia. In doing so, it should work for a neutralization of as much of that area as possible—not only the Indochina states, but Thailand as well and perhaps Burma. Outside parties to such a neutralization agreement should include China, the United States and the Soviet Union and possibly Japan, India and Pakistan. Its object would be to remove Southeast Asian states from the arena of great power conflict. At the very least, it would prohibit military ties between neutralized states and any outside power and eliminate all foreign bases and military personnel, including advisers, from them. At best, it would enjoin the neutralizing powers from giving military training to members of the armed forces of these countries outside as well as inside the area, provide for agreement among the neutralizing powers aimed at reducing the export of arms to the area, and arrange for inspection by an impartial outside body for the purpose of insuring that the provisions of the neutralization were carried out. In any case, it should be clearly understood that neutralization would be exclusively concerned with the external international context, and would not constitute an undertaking to stabilize the domestic political life of the Southeast Asian countries concerned or influence their political development.

Neutralization of continental Southeast Asia would conform with Peking's basic security interests. China's fear of encirclement would diminish, and she could be confident that as long as the neutralization of the Southeast Asian states adjacent to her was maintained, no hostile major power, whether the United States or Soviet Russia, could threaten her from bases within these countries. It is probable that Peking would find it in her own self interest to support such an arrangement and not undermine it by encouraging subversive actions against neighboring governments which, whatever their political cast, were prepared to adhere to this neutralization.

Chinese leaders cannot help but perceive that Peking's past efforts to influence her south-eastern security environment have for the most part failed. Encouragement of radicals and revolutionaries in several Southeast Asian countries has been largely ineffective in furthering China's security objectives, and more often than not actually counter-productive. For Peking to support subversive activity against a particular neutralized neighbor would, of course, run the risk of driving not only it but also adjoining states from neutrality into military ties with a power or powers unfriendly to China.

If it is argued that Peking finds the threat of encirclement of political advantage domestically (as a basis for unifying divergent factions), the threat of Soviet Russia alone should be sufficient. Peking is evidently uncomfortable at the prospect of an increasing Soviet presence in Southeast Asia. Along with increasing her fears of hostile encirclement, this would be likely to undermine her own influence with some non-communist as well as some communist elements. Because of Moscow's power and its much greater potential for economic aid, it appears to exert a stronger long-term attraction than Peking to most Asian communist leaders. China's greater commitment to revolutionary struggle is appreciated by some non-governing parties, but is not enough to align them with China, particularly once they have achieved governmental power.

Thus, communization of additional states in the area—improbable as this prospect is in the next decade—would not necessarily be a promising development for China. In view of the Sino-Soviet conflict it is unlikely that China would see either her security or ideological-revolutionary objectives advanced by the overthrow of non-communist or anti-communist "bourgeois" states in Southeast Asia if they are replaced by a series of Soviet communist allies. Perception of this long-range probability should influence China further in favor of an early neutralization of Southeast Asia. The spectre of increasing Soviet involvement in Southeast Asia implicitly linked to U.S. containment policies is likely to make a neutralization of the states of continental Southeast Asia all the more attractive to Peking.

****

The United States must distinguish much more sharply than in the past between invasion and internal subversion. The meaning of "subversion" has become so twisted in popular American usage as to inhibit an objective view of political processes abroad. Subversion is not the monopoly of the communists (after all the YMCA was regarded as "subversive" by the Imperial government of China), and it can be a healthy thing. It is as applicable to bad regimes as to good ones, to the overthrow of unrepresentative governments as to those that are representative. It should be recalled that the literal dictionary meaning of the word "subvert" is to "turn from beneath," and that its present primary definition is "to overturn or overthrow from the foundation." The majorities who constitute the social foundation of most Southeast Asian countries are sometimes oppressed by, and rarely effectively represented in, the governmental structures that rest on them. A change in the situation might well be socially and politically beneficial for them. The relationship of the United States with their present governments should not be of a nature that inhibits such a development.

The United States should be guided by the fact that no insurgency in Southeast Asia will be successful unless it reflects substantial popular support. If a government there cannot handle an insurgency on its own, that movement manifestly reflects considerable popular backing, of a magnitude probably as great if not greater than that enjoyed by the regime in power. The interposition of U.S. firepower (directly or by proxy) on the side of a government so beleaguered is more likely to prolong the fighting than determine its outcome.

6. Peace in Asia in the 1970s: Coexistence and Competition with the "Shadow of China"
MINEO NAKAJIMA

INTRODUCTION

The decade of the seventies should witness the emergence of a new international order based on new structural changes in post-war world politics. The cold war tensions of the bi-polarized post-war world, maintained by the Soviet-American nuclear power balance, began a rapid turn toward detente with the 1962 Cuban crisis. This change was brought about by the inherent contradictions in the balance system, and there emerged an era of multipolarization in world politics.

The road toward a Soviet-U.S. detente and multi-polarization was marked by the worsening dollar crisis in the United States, the tragic death of President Kennedy and the pathology of American society which produced such a tragedy, the Sino-Soviet rupture, the downfall of Khrushchev, Chinese nuclear armament, and disagreement between the "have" and the "have not" nations over the nuclear non-proliferation treaty. The challenging positions of nuclear-armed China and de Gaulle's nationalist France added to this trend toward multi-polarization.

In the closing year and a half of the decade of the sixties, there occurred many important international events which propelled world politics into a new era. These included the U.S. bombing halt against North Vietnam, the start of a U.S. military withdrawal from Vietnam, Soviet military intervention in Czechoslovakia, Sino-Soviet border clashes, the aftermath of the Chinese Great Cultural Revolution, the Ninth Chinese Communist Party Convention, and the retirement of General de Gaulle. These events of serious global implications, together with the mounting crisis in the international monetary system and social revolutions in the advanced countries, show clearly that the world is today moving into a new age. The shape of this new era is yet indistinct, but we are at least sure that we are facing a very important turning point in world history. What kind of peace for Asia is there to choose in the 1970s? I would suggest that the problem of dealing with China is central to any discussion of how to achieve peace in Asia.

THE U.S. "WITHDRAWAL" AND THE NEW ASIA

The March 31, 1968 statement of President Johnson can be compared, in a sense, to the January 1950 statement of non-intervention in Chinese affairs made by President Truman. The Johnson statement was apparently a reflection of a serious policy breakdown. Moreover, it symbolized the end of an era. The statement was not only a bitter admission of the U.S. failure to achieve its goal by sheer force, but even more significantly confirmed that nuclear might, which may be useful for maintaining the balance of power among big countries, is entirely useless against the bare-handed nationalistic revolutions of Asian people.

The United States is learning a multitude of lessons through its experience in the Vietnam war. These lessons, concisely summarized by Arthur Schlesinger, are: (1) Not all world events are equally important to the United States; (2) The United States cannot do everything in the world; (3) The United States cannot be the permanent and sole guarantor of security in this convulsive world; (4) Military force is not necessarily an effective indicator of a nation's power, and (5) The United States may, in the future, be able to wield a more effective influence by non-military means.

Today, the Vietnam policy of the Nixon Administration seems to be a stepped-up United States "retreat" from Vietnam, as promised by President Johnson. The June 25, 1969 Guam statement by President Nixon, who went on his Asian tour basking in the glory of the Apollo moon landing, hinted at a change in U.S. Asian policy. In his statement President Nixon declared that, after Vietnam, the United States would avoid direct military intervention in Asia, and that Asian conflicts should be solved by Asians themselves. This Nixon statement, as was observed by Senator Mansfield, is of such importance as to be called the "Guam Doctrine."

Change in American policy is particularly significant because it reflects a recognition of the need to improve Sino-American relations and the dialogue between the two countries. In this connection, it is significant that the United States Government, on July 21, immediately before Mr. Nixon's departure for his Asian tour, relaxed its restrictions on U.S. citizens' entry into China and purchases of Chinese-made products.

With the "retreat" of the United States, a new situation is coming into being in Asia. A complete U.S. withdrawal from Asia is impossible, but the United States is going to make major revisions in its policy of overcommitment in Asia. In the same way, Britain is ready to retreat "west of the Suez" after 1971. Such retreats by the major powers will create a vast power vacuum in Asia. Several years ago such a vacuum might have been filled by the solidarity of the newly-emerged and non-aligned Asian countries, or by such regional military alliances as CENTO and SEATO. Today, however, these substitutes for the presence of the major powers are no longer workable.

The Soviet Union has been most aggressive in seeking to fill this new Asian power vacuum. The Soviet Defense Minister visited India and Pakistan in March 1969; Premier

Kosygin called on India, Pakistan, and Afghanistan in May; and Soviet Communist Party Secretary Brezhnev suggested an Asian collective security system at the International Congress of Communist Parties in June. This proposed collective security system, though still highly ambiguous and too expressly directed against China, reflects Soviet intentions in post-Vietnam Asia.

Filling the Asian power vacuum to achieve peace and stability must involve means that have sound ties to the nationalism of the Asian people. The crucial question for peace in Asia is whether or not the outside world will accept the principle that it should not intervene to influence the course of social revolutions based on the nationalist aspirations of Asian peoples.

As America withdraws from Asia, the problems inherent in the countries of Asia will more clearly reveal themselves. The search for peace and stability in Asia will require the solution of many extremely complicated problems. These include racial and ethnic conflicts, politico-economic difficulties, opposition between revolutionary and anti-revolutionary forces, and different degrees of development among the countries. Also, new antagonisms and troubles will occur with religious and political problems, conflicts among local communities within countries, language barriers, industrialization, dictatorial political systems, and Chinese immigrants.

The failure of America's Asian policy may be traced to its being based upon a simple view of Asia as a victim of communist aggression, whereas the Asian situation is actually much more complex. Now Asia is going to face its own problems. This Asian agony is inevitable in the process of modernization and industrialization. To try to avoid such agony would be to remain forever a "developing" area of the world.

THE POST-VIETNAM ERA AND CHINA'S CULTURAL REVOLUTION

In the previous section, I touched upon the U.S. desire

to change its Asian policy and at the same time took note of the possibilities of a change in its policies toward China. Nevertheless, I do not think the United States will drastically change its China policy immediately. Consequently, we must always distinguish between this latent desire and political reality so as to be aware of the interrelation between them.

Needless to say, the basic thinking behind American China policy has been the idea of "containment." It has relied on the multiple use of legal, military, and economic means.

From a legal standpoint, readjustment in Sino-American relations can never be achieved until the United States, by legally recognizing China, establishes diplomatic relations and solves the problem of Chinese representation in the United Nations. Liberal elements in the United States have been strongly advocating change in American policy in this regard, but it appears unlikely that the U.S. Government will alter its present policies in the immediate future. For instance, President Nixon declared at his post-inaugural press conference that he would "continue to oppose Chinese participation in the United Nations." Solution of this issue is of course intimately related to the problem of Taiwan, but any change in U.S. policy toward Taiwan seems unlikely at present.

Secondly, let us consider the U.S. military response to China. The "anti-Chinese encirclement net" of U.S. conventional military forces may possibly weaken in the future, depending on changes in post-Vietnam Asia. Even if this were to happen, however, it is inconceivable that there would be any major change in American nuclear strategy. The U.S. position as the "nuclear policeman" or "holder of the nuclear umbrella" will not change. While the Johnson Administration's "Sentinel" program, which called for a thin ABM system to cope with anticipated Chinese ICBM development, has been altered by the Nixon Administration to the "Safeguard" project directed at the Soviet Union, and while the Administration's bill was finally passed by the Senate after long debate, it is still nevertheless true that American nuclear deployment continues to be directed toward China. As Chinese nuclear development approaches combat applicability, this issue will assume more serious proportions.

Finally, let us look at Chinese-American economic relations. The dollar crisis has produced an American desire to cut back on foreign aid. America is now asking those countries which have heretofore received aid to take over their own defense burdens. Under such conditions, the embargo on trade with China is being increasingly questioned in the United States. Change in U.S. economic policy toward China seems more likely than change in legal or military policies. Such change, however, will only take place if the U.S. feels that lifting the embargo against the Chinese economy, which is primarily agricultural and in light industries, will not threaten the world market.

Because of all these factors, it seems improbable that there will be any drastic changes in U.S. policies toward China in the near future. Such an assumption, of course, does not deny the latent American desire to change its policies. In the post-Vietnam era, the United States may move toward a policy of "containment without isolation" so as to facilitate communication with China. Yet, because of the growing Chinese nuclear capacity, the U.S. will continue to contain the Chinese "threat" militarily.

What, though, will be the situation for China? The logical explanation is that, as progress toward peace in Vietnam is likely to bring about an international environment favorable to China, the Chinese posture toward foreign countries under post-Vietnam conditions may well become more positive. At the Party's Ninth Congress China officially declared Soviet "socialist imperialism" its enemy. Due especially to a series of armed clashes along the Sino-Soviet border, China is trying to initiate a full-scale diplomatic strategy against the Soviet Union. The international isolation of China today is a far cry from China's avowed hope for international amity in the early days of its existence. Therefore, it is only a matter of course that Chinese diplomatic activities will move to normalize relations with such countries as France, Albania, Cambodia, Pakistan, North Vietnam, Tanzania, Guinea, Zambia, etc., with which China suspended diplomatic activities, symbolic of its "diplomacy of rebellion," amidst the Cultural Revolution. Its subtle maneuvers to approach Pakistan, Rumania, and Yugoslavia, however, are deserving of attention as part of a global anti-Soviet strategy which has already become China's highest national goal.

As these events imply, it is possible that China will gradually take a flexible attitude toward those nations which do not maintain close relations with Soviet revisionism. But this is not the result of progress toward peace in Vietnam. To be sure, some critics attribute the Cultural Revolution primarily to intensification of the Vietnam War. They see it as hastened political unification and military reorganization at home so as to be able to cope with a Chinese-American showdown, that is, with a direct attack by the United States. Those critics then surmise that China may now start a full-scale diplomatic offensive.

Such theorizing, however, ignores the fact that the Cultural Revolution basically originated from such internal factors as China's own political and social crisis during the process of making the "Thoughts of Mao Tse-tung" absolute, various problems during the period of economic readjustment after the failure of the 1958 Great Leap Forward, and the serious struggles within the Party caused by various issues in connection with Chinese foreign policy (especially its relations with the Soviet Union) during the first half of the 1960s. Insofar as the Cultural Revolution is basically the consequence of domestic factors, its struggles have been essentially unrelated to the Vietnam War. Consequently, the opening of Vietnam peace talks means a diplomatic failure for revolutionary China which has been urging North Vietnam to engage in a protracted struggle. China's position concerning peace in Vietnam and its failure to report even the facts about the continuation of the Paris peace talks give further testimony to the failure of Chinese policy. The effects of the Cultural Revolution on China's foreign policy and discord with Hanoi on a Vietnam peace have represented serious diplomatic setbacks. As a result, the base for developing a positive diplomacy in post-Vietnam Asia has to embody the ideals of the Great Cultural Revolution. China may have no other choice but to push forward the "Liu Shao-chi line without Liu Shao-chi."

However, the important exception here is Chinese strategy against the Soviet Union. China has begun to regard the Soviet Union as a strategic enemy not only ideologically and politically but militarily as well. Under these circumstances the series of Sino-Soviet border clashes gave China an excellent chance for strategic and ideological indoctrination to convince its 700 million people to change their image of the Soviet Union and see it as "Chinese Public Enemy Number 1." Since the border incident on Damansky Island in the Ussuri River, more than 400 million Chinese have taken part in organized demonstrations throughout the country. This is an indication of the nationwide campaign to change the image of the Soviet Union. Furthermore, the Soviet Union is the only country against which China can make the charge of revisionism, and thereby transform one of the fundamental ideas of the Great Cultural Revolution into policy. As a matter of fact, since the Soviet armed intervention in Czechoslovakia last summer, Chinese leaders have been loudly voicing the possibility of a direct invasion of China by Soviet "Socialist Imperialism," and appear seriously concerned with such a possibility. The fact that the armed intervention in Czechoslovakia was made by a sudden attack by Soviet tanks must also have been a serious blow to those Chinese leaders whose theories are based on long People's Wars of attrition. A joint editorial entitled "No Enemy Anywhere can Withstand the Libration Army: In Commemoration of the 42nd Anniversary of the Foundation of the Chinese People's Liberation Army" in the *China People's Daily, Red*

Flag, and *Liberation Army Bulletin* on August 1, 1969, appealed to the Chinese people to be ready in the event of direct aggression against China by the United States or the Soviet Union. The editorial indicates the distrust with which the Chinese leaders view the Soviet Union.

Now, let us direct our attention to the situation within China. The Party's Ninth Congress held in April of 1969 revealed that the Mao-Lin structure has been established throughout China. On the other hand, the task of reconstructing the Chinese Communist Party, completely demolished by the Great Cultural Revolution, has yet to be done, and the reconstruction of the Party from below has had to be postponed. There are, of course, many problems to be discussed in the relationship between the Ninth Congress and the Great Cultural Revolution. What kind of political position within the system is to be given in the future to the revolutionary committees, which are a direct product of the power struggle? How should the sharp contradiction between the desire to attain order and structure for the reconstruction and unification of the Party on the one hand, and the desire to destroy and disrupt that which has been planned by the already extinct spirit of "righteous rebellion" on the other be met? How may solutions be found to the historic problems of Chinese society—reform of the vast agrarian society and modernization and industrialization—in the face of tremendous population pressure? What kind of reform should be established in Chinese society after the Great Cultural Revolution? Although these and many other problems are exceedingly important, none was taken up in either the new Party rules or Lin Piao's political report. Despite its intense belligerence Lin's report completely ignored any concrete measures for national construction. Even the third five year program was not mentioned. This leads one to suspect that the Chinese leaders themselves are perhaps unable to exercise full control over these basic issues. It therefore seems that China, in the short run, cannot but give priority to domestic policies of national reconstruction and unity.

Consequently, China probably cannot afford for some time to develop dynamic foreign policies in conformity with the ideas of the Great Cultural Revolution, and it is for this reason that they cannot but advance the "Liu Shao-chi line without Liu Shao-chi." The only country toward which foreign policy can conform with such domestic policies as "self-struggle to criticize revisionism" and criticisms of "capitalist factions" without requiring great diplomatic efforts is the Soviet Union. In this respect, too, it may be said that the Sino-Soviet confrontation is moving forward into a more serious stage.

In this light the Sino-American relationship may be seen as entering a new phase in which the U.S. tends to a neo-isolationism and China to a policy of giving first priority to domestic politics, that is, to a self-imposed isolationism. Consequently we must forecast gradual but major changes in the Sino-American confrontation that has characterized the postwar period. It is only by looking objectively at the undercurrents propelling Asia in this new direction that we can hope to have any control in the quest for Asian peace and security.

THE CHINA THREAT AND "THE SHADOW OF CHINA"

An estimation of the so-called "China threat" is prerequisite to any search for Asian peace. Until now, of course, the view that China does represent a real threat has dominated government thinking in both Japan and the United States. For example, the Sato-Johnson joint communique on the occasion of Prime Minister Sato's visit to the United States in November of 1967 did not make clear the meaning of the China threat but emphasized defense efforts to resist it. But efforts to respond to a threat that is not clearly defined and understood can only aggravate tensions. We must first, therefore, analyze the meaning of the "China threat."

Generally, three elements are involved when people talk

of the China threat. The first is the threat brought about by the Chinese strategy of global revolution, the second is China's diplomatic threat, and the third is China's nuclear threat. These three elements are intertwined with each other, but for purposes of analysis it is useful to examine them separately.

The Chinese strategy for global revolution, which has become particularly clear since the Sino-Soviet conflict, emphasizes armed national liberation struggles in the underdeveloped nations of Asia, Africa, and Latin America. It is a strategy that is built upon a complete denial of the possibility of peaceful revolutionary change in advanced nations and one that looks forward to the victory of armed national liberation struggles in the underdeveloped "world's countryside" leading to the encirclement of the "world's cities," especially the United States. The strategy universalizes the unique Chinese Yenan experience and Mao Tsetung's views of revolutionary uprisings. Yet this strategy for global revolution has suffered severe setbacks within the Afro-Asian bloc since 1965 (the failure of the September 30 *coup d'etat* in Indonesia, the miscarriage of the Second Afro-Asian Conference, and failures in various African nations). China became isolated even within those Afro-Asian nations which are in its own strategic zone. Lin Piao's thesis "Long Live the Victory of the People's Wars" in September of 1965 described the strategy of aggressive encirclement "from the world's countryside to the world's cities" and attempted to show China's position as the base for world revolution. But, despite the belligerent language, this was an admission of the inability of China to give concrete substance to its strategy of global revolution. The intensification of the Great Cultural Revolution and the isolation of China within the international communist movement accelerated China's retreat from active efforts to foster its strategy of global revolution. Even the Vietnam Workers Party sharply criticized the Lin Piao strategy and the Great Cultural Revolution. The 1967 anti-British riots in Hong Kong sharply revealed the contradictions between

China's revolutionary principles and its national interest. Even in Mao's revolutionary China the latter won out.

Obviously China's strategy of global revolution has run into major problems regarding the methods for "exporting revolution." But more than anything the geopolitical assumptions upon which it is based are so weak as to make it incapable of providing a realistic approach to resolving the contradictions of the present world. There is no evidence to support the contention that the China "threat" of global revolution represents a real threat.

The second element of the China threat, the diplomatic threat, is intimately related to the strategy of global revolution. An outstanding characteristic of China's diplomatic practice is that, while in principle maintaining a line that is consistent with the strategy of global revolution, it exercises considerable flexibility in foreign policy. In a sense it has much more maneuverability than the Soviet Union. The Soviet Union's major concern in world politics is to prevent international disputes from developing into thermonuclear war. This not only greatly restricts its foreign policy but constantly exposes the contradictions between its great power role and its position as a socialist nation having to stand on the side of revolutionary justice in national wars of liberation. China, on the other hand, does not face these restrictions on policy or the contradictions with principle they produce. It maintains the freedom to develop nuclear weapons and determine foreign policy as it sees fit.

China's diplomatic strategy may be thought by some to be a major threat. The dynamic development of the Five Principles of Peace diplomacy proved effective in dealing with international situations surrounding the emergence of Afro-Asian nations. For those who would block this historic development the "shadow of China" was an extraordinary threat. It needs to be stressed that China's relative freedom of choice in deciding foreign policy raises the issue of the decisive influence of domestic politics in determining foreign policy. In the competitive and complementary relationship between domestic politics and foreign policy, the influence of domestic politics is greater than general active principles of foreign policy. China's present preoccupation with achieving internal order leaves no room for the development of a dynamic foreign policy notably different from the "Liu Shao-chi line without Liu Shao-chi." This accordingly diminishes rather considerably the threat of Chinese diplomacy.

Though the Chinese strategy of global revolution and its diplomatic line do not necessarily add up to a substantive threat, there is the issue of Chinese nuclear weapons.

At present, while the ideal of establishing a non-nuclear world order is struggling for acceptance, China prides itself on its refusal to accept any restraints on its nuclear development and boasts of its determination to destroy the Soviet-American nuclear monopoly. Chinese nuclear development continued to be promoted during the Great Cultural Revolution with only a bare minimum of disruption. From the perspective of Chinese thinking on nuclear proliferation and its desire that Japan break its relationship with the United States, China, as some people have been saying recently, might even favor nuclear arms for Japan. Yonosuke Nagai, for example, has speculated that "from the Chinese viewpoint, the arming of Japan perhaps should be welcomed in certain political contexts."[1]

There are people in Japan who urge the development of an independent Japanese nuclear force to meet the Chinese nuclear challenge. But we must ask if it really makes any sense to try to deal with Chinese nuclear weapons on a "fight fire with fire" basis. Because this problem is so serious, we must try to analyze objectively the political meaning of Chinese nuclear weapons.

After the Chinese successfully exploded a nuclear bomb in October of 1964, the same time that Soviet Premier Khrushchev was being dismissed, Chou En-lai spoke of the test saying, "Did not we explode an atomic bomb? Have

[1]"The 'Balance of Power' in Asia": *Economist*: Tokyo; 1968 Special New Year's Edition.

not we thrown off the nickname of the invalids of the Orient given us by the people of Western Europe? How can anyone think that the proletariat of the East are unable to do whatever the bourgeoisie of the West can do?"[2] This Chou En-lai statement reflects the intensity of the national ambition which produced the Chinese struggle for nuclear development.

How, though, does China, having pursued nuclear development against this background, evaluate its practical nuclear capacity? While the formula, "people's wars over atomic bombs" is a well-known program, the Chinese Communist Party today persists in emphasizing that "in building missiles with our own strength and striking a serious blow against the nuclear monopoly of the Soviet Union and the United States, we are giving great inspiration and encouragement to peoples carrying out heroic revolutionary struggles which continue to advance throughout the world. Yet in the future, too, we must defeat our enemies in people's wars."[3]

This statement reflects a dual strategic concept of recognizing the supremacy of the "people over weapons" logic of people's wars, while unreservedly emphasizing the militant "fight nuclear weapons with nuclear weapons" aspect of Mao Tse-tung's military thought. Moreover, it must be remembered that this thinking was not born of such external factors as the existence of the "anti-Chinese encirclement net" but was a product of internal factors. It was the logical extension of the Chinese Communist Party's theoretical view of the world today. Thus the development of nuclear weapons by China should not be considered as merely a military matter. There are other reasons, such as the desire to prove themselves equal to the West that have led the Chinese to develop a nuclear capacity. In fact Lin

[2] Political Activities Report at the First National People's Delegates Conference of the Third Period.

[3] "Let us Study 'Strategic Problems of the Chinese Revolution' by Mao Tse-tung": *Liberation Army Report*; December 29, 1966.

Piao's above-mentioned essay on people's wars is premised on the impossibility of nuclear war, and develops a strategy for drawing enemies onto the Chinese mainland and developing people's wars. It is imperative that we understand the paradox of China's nuclear challenge. It is quite clear, even if we leave aside China's avowal that it will never make a nuclear first strike, that the Chinese nuclear challenge does not immediately mean a military threat.

From the examination of these three elements, we can see that there is a real danger that the so-called Chinese threat may be over-estimated and greatly misread, depending upon the ideological illusions of the viewer. People shouting about the China threat may be reacting in fact to the "shadow of China."

ASIAN PEACE AND JAPANESE DIPLOMACY

While I have tried in the above to examine the Chinese threat, I am not one to deny the threat entirely. But I feel the threat of China exists in a different dimension.

As the Great Cultural Revolution clearly shows, China today is in a state of total ideological commitment to making absolute "the thoughts of Mao Tse-tung," and building a charismatic, patriarchial system of support for Mao upon the fanatic emotions of the masses which are sweeping the entire land. China, intentionally trying to establish a self-contained autarchal society, is rejecting the pragmatic approach to modern society through industrialization, and is molding a society ruled by political myth.

The real threat of China is its internal condition, a kind of "state of the masses" completely cut off from the outside world, embracing within it 700 million people, being incapable even now of breaking out of its social and economic backwardness, and slowly developing nuclear weapons. That such a China should fill the wide spaces of continental Asia is itself an acute threat to the peace of Asia. This is because, should this "state of the masses" once lose its internal equilibrium, it is liable to explode and become reckless in all directions. And this is a nuclear-armed state. That is why it is now time for the rest of the world seriously to consider developing policies that will not force China further in this direction. For this purpose, it is imperative that concrete steps be devised to fill the present frightening gap between China and the outside world and bring China into international society.

We must patiently and tenaciously seek coexistence with this colossus. The issue of Chinese representation in the United Nations is of crucial importance in this regard. It is particularly important now that Japanese diplomacy undertake a concerted effort to prepare positive alternative proposals to its policy of designating the problem of Chinese representation an "important question." America, now groping for a fundamental change in its Asian policies, is expecting much of Japan, and the Soviet Union also is making approaches to Japan as never before. Diplomatically, Japan may be said to be in a "seller's market." Rather than making do with makeshift measures, it should in its independence boldly mark out a new diplomacy of peace to cope with the new situation in Asia. The time is passing when Japan can pursue only its own national interests under a cheap-for-Japan security system. Establishing such an independent Japanese diplomacy would shortly, even if the China problem is converted into merchandise with which to bargain with America, push Japanese diplomacy directly in the direction of coexistence with China which would, in turn, foster Asian peace and security.

China is now strongly critical of Japan for taking over the American policy of containing China, and is accusing Japan of trying to establish a new "anti-Chinese encirclement net" in cooperation with the Soviet Union. It is also suspicious of Japan's economic expansion into Asian nations. While it is not necessary for us to accept Chinese criticisms at face value, it is important that we reflect deeply upon the fact that Japan is incapable of exerting an influence commensurate with its economic strength in conducting a diplomacy of peace. Some tensions and frictions may well arise in our relations with America should Japanese diplomacy seek actively for accommodation with China. But it is unrealistic to think that Japan and the United States can eternally maintain their alliance in its present form. Japan, as a responsible Asian state, should propose Asian-oriented diplomatic policies to America. It is in this form that the true friendship and ideal of the Japanese-American relationship ought to be sought.

Efforts gradually to overcome the various bad effects of the hardening of the U.S.-Japan security system must also be made. If America is trying fundamentally to change its Asian policy, revisions will have to be made in its policies toward Japan as well. The biggest problem for us, however, is the idleness of the Japanese government. The government has failed to develop alternative policies that can lead the United States in groping toward new Asian policies and relations with China. The various opposition parties, naturally, must also bear some responsibility for this situation. Japan must make a concerted effort to bring itself and lead others away from dealing with the "shadow of China," and create policies for improving relations with the real China and improving the chances for Asian and world peace.

7. *American Policy Toward Japan in the Seventies: The Need for Disengagement*

GERALD L. CURTIS

LOOKING INTO THE FUTURE

There is a Japanese saying that "The devil laughs at those who talk about what will happen next year." The authors of the papers in this volume have attempted to talk not only of next year, but of the coming decade. Indeed, events may set the devil laughing at all of us and our predictions, hopes and premonitions. Nonetheless, if foreign policy is to be anything more than a makeshift response to immediate events, an attempt must be made to anticipate the future.

Although each of the writers has addressed himself to a different aspect of the future of Japanese-American relations, certain common assumptions about the coming decade emerge. All assume, for instance, increased American attention to domestic problems and a cautious attitude toward further military intervention in Southeast Asia. They predict for Japan continued high economic growth rates and, partly as a consequence, a desire for a more influential role in international relations. They assume that the dissatisfactions of youth, the existence of poverty amidst increasing affluence, and the frustrations of the individual in an ever more computerized technological society are problems that will be of increasing concern to both the United States and Japan. In regard to Japanese-American relations in particular the theme that clearly emerges is that the 1970's will open a "new era."

This concluding paper relates these themes to developments in American policy toward Japan. What kind of policies can best meet the needs of the "new era" of the seventies? What kind of political relationship does the United States want with Japan, and what international role does it want to encourage Japan to play? What changes in American policy are required to strengthen the political base of the relationship and improve the chances for peace in Asia?

In order to better gaze into the new era of the seventies, we should first briefly look back at the course of Japanese-American relations since the end of the Pacific War. American objectives *vis-a-vis* Japan have not remained constant over this quarter of a century, and changed objectives have at times required major readjustments. In terms of objectives, American policy toward Japan since 1945 can be divided into three eras.

THE FIRST ERA

The first part of the Occupation of Japan, from 1945 to about the beginning of 1948, marks the boundaries of the first era. The overriding American objective in this period was to insure that Japan would never again become a threat to international peace. American policy, as executed through the Occupation authorities, aimed broadly at the demilitarization and democratization of the country. The assumption behind these policies was that demilitarization would make Japan physically incapable of aggression and democratization would destroy the source of aggression, rooted, as the Occupiers saw it, in Japan's social structure. The adoption of a Constitution which denied the right of belligerency, guaranteed civil rights, established full parliamentary authority, and reduced the Emperor to the position of a "symbol of the State," was characteristic of this period. Other measures such as land and educational reforms and the breakup of the *zaibatsu* were also imposed by the Occupation authorities to achieve the objective of creating a peaceful, democratic Japan.

In formulating its immediate postwar policy toward Japan, the United States assumed continued friendly relations with its wartime allies. But as relations with the Soviet Union grew more tense, and the inability of the Chiang Kai-shek regime to defeat the Communist Chinese armies grew more apparent, the basic premises of United States policy toward Japan were brought into question. The reformist zeal that characterized policy toward Japan in the years immediately following the war was dampened by 1948. With the fall of Czechoslovakia in that year and the victory of Mao Tse-tung in the next, American objectives toward Japan underwent a fundamental change. The goal of American policy became insuring Japan's participation in America's alliance system. This objective characterized the second era in Japanese-American relations that was to last about a decade, from 1948 to 1957.

THE SECOND ERA

To achieve its objective in this period, the United States undertook several policies of particular importance. One was to make the conclusion of a peace treaty contingent on the signing of a bilateral security pact that would insure the free use of Japan as a base for American military operations in the Far East. The second was to continue American control of Okinawa and the Bonin Islands. The third was to press Japan to rearm. The fourth was to aid Japanese economic reconstruction.

On September 8, 1951, a peace treaty was signed with Japan by the United States and 48 of its Allies. The Soviet Union took part in the peace conference but refused to sign the treaty. The result was a "separate peace" that left Japan technically at war with America's new enemies and closely tied to American foreign policy.

Later on the same day Japan and the United States signed a bilateral Security Treaty. This gave the United States the right to station troops in Japan and use them anywhere in the Far East. There was no specific obligation to defend Japan. Japan could not grant bases to a third power without United States permission and no provision was made for any Japanese say in the use of American bases in Japanese territory. The details of the base agreement were to be made in a separate administrative agreement that did not need Diet approval. The United States, at the request of the Japanese Government, could act to put down internal disturbances in Japan. No time limit was set on the treaty. The preamble referred to American forces in Japan as a "provisional arrangement" and called upon Japan to rearm.

The peace and security treaties were largely the work of John Foster Dulles, who was appointed Foreign Policy Adviser to the Secretary of State in April, 1950 with special responsibility for arriving at a peace settlement with Japan. Dulles was convinced that Japan had only two options in its role in the international system. It could choose to enter the ranks of the Western democracies or it could choose communist domination. The suspicion and contempt for neutralism for which Dulles was to be noted when he served as Secretary of State were already evident in his attitude toward a peace settlement with Japan. In a speech he made in Tokyo in June of 1950, a speech appropriately entitled "The Free World and the Captive World," Dulles declared: "As the surrender terms are fulfilled, Japan's destiny will increasingly be in her own hands. Japan would have the opportunity of choosing between the Free World and the Captive World. In making this choice the Japanese will determine their future destiny."

Although Dulles was determined to avoid the experience of Versailles, forcing upon the vanquished a punitive peace that could only further embitter relations, his view of Japan's role in a bi-polar world precluded any settlement that would have given Japan the freedom to choose anything but alliance with the United States. One can argue that the conservative leadership which has ruled Japan almost continuously since the end of the war would not have opted for neutralism (as it was being urged to do by the nation's "progressive intellectuals") and that it saw alliance with the United States as serving Japan's national interest. Nonetheless the fact remains that for a very large number of Japanese the original Security Treaty was viewed as involving Japan against her will in the Cold War, compromising Japanese sovereignty and achieving a semi-occupation of Japan by the United States. The peace and security treaties came into effect, and the Occupation came to an end, on April 28, 1952. Demands for the revision or abolition of the Security Treaty were to be in the forefront of Japanese political struggles for the rest of this second period.

A second major policy in this period was to keep Okinawa under the direct rule of the United States Department of Defense. Repeatedly the United States indicated its recognition of Japanese "residual sovereignty" over Okinawa, but maintained that the islands could be returned only when conditions made the American military presence there unnecessary. In November 1953, then Vice President Richard Nixon stated that the United States would keep Okinawa as along as a communist threat existed in Asia. In his 1954 State of the Union Address, President Eisenhower affirmed that the United States would keep Okinawa "indefinitely." No significant move was made to give the nearly one million inhabitants of Okinawa a voice in the governing of the islands until the very end of the period. In June 1957 President Eisenhower issued an executive order defining the administrative organization of the islands and providing for a unicameral legislature. All legislation, however, was subject to the veto of the American High Commissioner.

The third major policy in this period was to encourage the Japanese Government to undertake a large scale rearmament program. In negotiating the peace settlement, Dulles insisted that the stationing of American troops on Japanese soil was a provisional arrangement; that Japan had to rearm and that the United States could not give Japan a "free ride" on its security indefinitely. Shortly after the outbreak of the Korean War in July 1950, General MacArthur ordered the Japanese Government to establish a National Police Reserve of 75,000 men. The force was expanded to 110,000 men with the coming into effect of the Peace Treaty, and paved the way for the establishment of a Defense Agency and a Self Defense Force in July 1954.

Japanese calls for revision of the Security Treaty, which increased as Japan recovered economically, were rebuffed by the United States. When Foreign Minister Shigemitsu went to Washington in 1955 to suggest treaty revision, Dulles demanded a tremendous increase in Japanese troop strength. Large scale rearmament was the *quid pro quo* demanded by the United States for treaty revision or the return of American occupied Japanese territory.

The fourth policy of note in this period, particularly in its early years, was American efforts to aid Japanese economic reconstruction, efforts motivated by the belief that economic progress was necessary for political stability and that the rebuilding of Japanese strength was essential for America's strategic interests in Asia. During the "reverse course" of American policy in the later years of the Occupation, emphasis was placed on extending economic and technical aid, slowing down or ending many of the reforms of preceding years, and lobbying among its allies to keep restrictions on the armament industry and shipbuilding out of the peace treaty, and the amount of reparations to a minimum. Of course, the Korean War provided an enormous boost to the Japanese economy, which thereafter continued to grow at an ever-increasing tempo and rendered direct American aid unnecessary.

The shift in American objectives and policies from the first to the second period was viewed by Americans as being necessitated by the Cold War. Many found it impossible to understand how the Japanese could feel otherwise.

The United States was protecting Japan from an aggressive communist bloc, and Japan should face up to the facts of international life, increase its defense capabilities and play a more positive role in defending the free world. The Japanese, ever since the beginning of the second period, have been accused by Americans of being "unrealistic" for maintaining a constitutional limitation on the right to have armed forces and for supporting other policies originally forced upon them by the United States in the name of democracy in the early years of the Occupation.

For the Japanese, on their part, it was inevitable that the economic and spiritual recovery of the nation would result in a strong demand for revision of the Security Treaty. There had of course been a significant element of the population opposed from the beginning to the Security Treaty and the "separate peace" with the United States and its allies. Dissatisfaction with the Treaty increased in Japan throughout the period as more and more people became convinced that it prevented Japan from being fully independent and threatened to involve the country in a war of American making.

Toward the end of the second period the Japanese Government repeatedly requested the opening of negotiations to revise the Treaty. It was not until Dulles passed from the scene, however, that treaty revision came to be seriously considered in Washington. The first official negotiations on revision were begun in Tokyo in October 1958. These negotiations paved the way for the opening of the third era in postwar Japanese-American relations.

THE THIRD ERA

The objective of American policy in the third period was more ambiguous than in previous years. Although Japanese participation in the United States' alliance system was still regarded as vital to American interests, greater emphasis was placed than before on respecting Japanese views, changing policies that were particularly irritating to Japan and moving toward "partnership" rather than American domination. Unlike the dramatic shift in objectives in the late forties, the shift in the late fifties and early sixties was gradual and moderate.

A first hint of a new period in American policy toward Japan came in the Kishi-Eisenhower communique of 1957, which referred to a "new era" in Japanese-American relations. The establishment at that time of a joint committee to study problems relating to the Security Treaty was one indication of American willingness to consider treaty revision, and the communique's statement that the United States would consult where practicable with Japan regarding the "disposition and employment in Japan by the United States of its forces" pointed to eventual agreement on prior consultation. On the other hand, no indication was given that the United States might consider responding to Japanese desires for the return of Okinawa. The communique stated flatly that "so long as the conditions of threat or tension exist in the Far East, the United States will find it necessary to continue the present status."

Japanese Government demands for a revision of the most objectionable provisions of the Security Treaty, backed by strong public demands for greater Japanese control over its own foreign policy, resulted in the signing on January 19, 1960 of the Treaty of Mutual Cooperation and Security between the United States of America and Japan and an accompanying exchange of notes. The Treaty, which came into effect on June 23, 1960, represented an important revision of the earlier Treaty in specifically obligating the United States to meet the common danger "in case of armed attack on either party in the territories under the administration of Japan", eliminating the clause on internal riots, and limiting the original term of the treaty to ten years, after which it could be abrogated by either party one year after giving offical notice of the intention to abrogate. A separate exchange of notes provided for prior consultation concerning major changes in the deployment, equipment and use of United States bases in Japan for combat operations outside the country.

Throughout the period there were moves to put the relationship on a more equal basis. The appointment of Edwin Reischauer as Ambassador and the importance attached to opening a "dialogue" with Japan set a new tone for the period. Although the United States continued to press Japan to make greater efforts in its military defense, it gradually retreated from making this a *quid pro quo* for the return of Okinawa and other Japanese territory. In March 1962 President Kennedy referred to Okinawa as part of the Japanese "homeland" and stressed America's hope for eventual reversion. Shortly thereafter a United States-Japan Committee to coordinate the economic assistance programs of the two countries in Okinawa was established. As a result of the first Sato-Johnson meeting of January 1965, the scope of activities of the Joint Committee was broadened to include "other matters" which would promote the welfare of the inhabitants. The second Sato-Johnson meeting, in November 1967, resulted in the return to Japan of the Bonin Islands and a promise to study the Okinawan issue "with a view to the return of administrative rights to Japan." Throughout 1969 negotiations were held on the conditions and timing of Okinawan reversion.

THE "NEW ERA"

It seems clear that we are now entering a new era. As the other articles in this volume have stressed, changes in the structure of the international political system, as well as domestic developments in both the United States and Japan, are presenting new opportunities and imposing new constraints on Japanese and American foreign policies. As the decade of the seventies unfolds, it is important to take a new look at the question of American objectives *vis-a-vis* Japan and the policies that can best achieve them.

A basic problem surrounding discussion of the future of Japanese-American relations is the lack of a clear consensus in the United States on what our objectives should be. On the one hand Americans realize the vital importance of maintaining friendly relations with Japan and recognize that the security of Japan is by far our most important interest in Asia. Yet on the other hand, past eras exert a strong influence on our perception of objectives and sometimes result in policies that are irrelevant or harmful in a changed environment.

The basic objective of American policy should be the maintenance of friendly relations with a democratic, peaceful and prosperous Japan. In the world of the 1970's the achievement of this objective requires the establishment of a new balance between political and military interests in American policy. General developments in American foreign policy, domestic pressures in the United States and the desires of the Japanese, taken together, point to the need for a considerable degree of disengagement in the Japanese-American relationship. In some ways the bear hug in which the United States and Japan have been joined in the past years needs to be loosened.

VIETNAM AND JAPANESE-AMERICAN RELATIONS

American policy toward Japan in the coming years will be intimately connected with developments in the Vietnam war. Unless the war is brought to an end or, at the least, American participation in it is ended, relations with Japan can only become more tense. The war has taken a tremendous toll in human lives and resources and in public confidence both in the United States and abroad, and in Japan has resulted in increased anti-Americanism.

An ending of American participation in the Vietnam conflict is likely to have three consequences that will bear heavily on the course of United States policy toward Japan. One is the strong possibility for a reduction in America's commitments to come to the military aid of beleaguered Southeast Asian regimes. A second is the growth of isolationism in the United States. The third is the likelihood of

increasing demands in the United States for its Asian allies
to carry more of the burden for the defense of the region.
It is clear today that most Americans want to get out of
Vietnam, in one fashion or another. Yet it is not at all
clear what lessons Americans, and most particularly the
Administration, are drawing from the Vietnam conflict. If
one lesson learned is that the United States should not
interfere in what are essentially domestic insurrections, the
likelihood in the coming decade is for a generally more
cautious attitude toward military involvement in Southeast
Asia. A general withdrawal from Southeast Asia would of
course encourage a reconsideration of some of our policies
toward Japan, for example, a reappraisal of the need for an
extensive base structure in Okinawa and in Japan's main
islands.

It is not entirely clear however that this is the lesson the
United States is bringing back from Vietnam. Administration statements of an intention to reduce the American
presence in Southeast Asia are coupled with statements
such as the one President Nixon made in the summer of
1969 in Thailand to the effect that the United States
would aid that country's regime against its enemies, both
internal and external. If American policy makers continue
to regard international politics in Asia in terms of a confrontation between the "free world" (a term which requires
quite a stretching of the imagination to apply to some of
our Asian allies) and Chinese communism and continue to
emphasize military intervention in the area, Japanese-
American relations are likely to enter a period of conflict
unprecedented in the postwar period. There is a very real
danger that using Japan as a base for military activities
elsewhere in the Far East and urging Japan to play a more
active military role will undermine the political foundation
on which the Japanese-American alliance rests.

The pressures for continued military involvement in
Southeast Asia created by Administration assumptions
about the relationship of the *status quo* there to American
security interests will be considerably weakened by the

anti-interventionist trend presently visible in important
sectors of Congressional and public opinion.

Congressional attempts to reestablish civilian control over
the military establishment and cut down on military spending will increase in the coming years. Public demands for a
reordering of national priorities to tackle the issues of
poverty, racism, urban ills and other domestic problems will
also grow and with them a demand for a reduction in
American commitments overseas and a cutback in military
and aid spending. An Administration concerned with maintaining public support will be extremely sensitive to these
trends and is not likely to undertake foreign commitments
that clearly contravene them.

Insofar as these developments lead to a reconsideration
of America's real security interests in Asia and the rest of
the world, they will prove beneficial to American relations
with Japan. The danger, however, is that such sentiment
will result in the emergence of a neo-isolationsim that
would adversely affect our relations with Japan and other
important allies.

TOTAL INVOLVEMENT VERSUS TOTAL ISOLATION

Although the emergence of isolationism in the sixties has
been popularly associated with leftist opposition to the
Vietnam war, the call for isolationism in the seventies may
very well come increasingly from the right. Although some
critics on the left appear to deny any significant international role for the United States, the general criticism of
the left has not been directed against international involvement as such but against a foreign policy that places undue
emphasis on the use of military force.

The growth of isolationist sentiment among those sectors
of the public that have most fervently supported American
military intervention in the past is a very real danger.
Internationalism for many such Americans has primarily
meant the use of American military power around the
globe to prevent communist regimes, whether by external

aggression or internal revolution, from coming to power. For many the only alternative to this role is creating a garrison state and letting others "stew in their own juice." Such an alternative will be attractive particularly in regard to American involvement in Asia. Frustration over Vietnam and a general loss of confidence in the ability of the United States to achieve its objectives in the area are likely to reinforce sentiments for a total withdrawal.

There is a tendency for many Americans to treat total involvement and isolationism as two sides of the same coin. In the debate in the United States over Okinawa, for instance, some of the political leaders who have taken the hardest line on the reversion issue have argued that if the United States cannot maintain free use of the bases in Okinawa it should pull out of Japan all together. The Japanese need us more than we need them. If they do not want to allow our military to carry out its responsibilities as it sees fit, Japan can go and take care of itself. Such an argument reveals an inability to consider the broad range of alternatives that mark the spectrum from isolationism to total, military-oriented, involvement. Regrettably this inability is all too widespread in American society. It is a legacy of America's historic experience of swinging from the one extreme of isolationism in the interwar period to total worldwide involvement following World War Two. Neither of these polar opposites can meet the needs of the seventies. The challenge for the United States is to carve out a foreign policy that represents a responsible internationalism.

JAPANESE MILITARY POWER AND AMERICAN POLICY

Americans often exhibit an exasperation with Japan's foreign policies. Japan is wealthy but uses less than one percent of its gross national product for military expenses. It relies on America for its security but refuses to play any role in the defense of its neighbors. It refuses to allow the

United States unfettered use of military bases in Japan and demands the return of Okinawa under conditions that would seriously hamper American military activities in the Asian area. It maintains an unrealistic constitutional prohibition against belligerency and the right to build armed forces. Japan has been getting a "free ride" on its security and now must show more "responsibility" and carry a fair share of the burden for the defense of itself and its neighbors.

The argument that Japan has not done enough in its own defense does not stand up under examination. In spite of the constitutional prohibition on military forces specified in Article Nine and a public opinion that is strongly anti-military, Japan has a military establishment of over a quarter of a million men equipped with highly sophisticated conventional weaponry.

Japanese defense expenditures in 1969 amounted to 1.344 billion dollars, and they have been increasing by 100 to 150 million dollars annually over the past decade. At the present rate of increase, these will reach three billion dollars by 1975, making Japan sixth or seventh in the world in terms of absolute dollar outlay for military purposes.

Some Americans and Japanese argue that Japan is not spending enough on its military establishment. They point out that only 0.84% of Japan's GNP was used for military purposes in 1969 compared to nearly ten percent for the United States. Indeed the percentage of GNP used for military purposes has been decreasing throughout the past decade. For many of the proponents of a stronger Japanese military establishment, a figure of two percent of GNP has become something of a magic number for a proper level of military expenditures.

Relating Japanese military expenditures to percentage of GNP has little relevance in a country where annual economic growth rates are over ten percent. Annual military expenditures have been increasing at a high rate despite a decrease in the percentage of GNP allocated to them. An increase in military expenditures to two percent would provide more money than can be rationally used unless Japan undertakes an ambitious nuclear weapons development program, a development the American Government apparently opposes and one that would raise enormous domestic problems in Japan.

All too often arguments about Japanese defense expenditures are conducted without reference to the basic question: what is Japan to defend? There is little sense of external threat in Japan. Indeed the most generally perceived threat is the indirect one presented by the United States, which could involve Japan in a conflict not of its own choosing.

At its present strength the Japanese Self Defense Forces could deal with a small scale conventional attack. But, more importantly, a military attack against Japan or military interference with Japan's sea or air routes would represent a direct threat to the interests of the United States. Self sufficiency in military defense will not be any more possible in the world of the seventies than in the world of the sixties. As long as the American commitment to defend Japan remains credible, there is no reason in terms of American interests, for any major increase in Japanese military strength.

American encouragement for such an increase, it seems to me, is based upon an unrealistic assessment of the forces at work in contemporary Japanese society. Any concerted effort by Japan to increase its military capabilities would run counter to American interests. It ultimately would lead to the possession of nuclear weapons and would be motivated by a nationalism directed largely against the United States.

In spite of Japan's "nuclear allergy," there has been growing sympathy among conservatives in Japan for the development of a nuclear capability, and a marked increase in the number of Japanese who expect Japan to have nuclear weapons in the seventies. A de Gaulle style *force de frappe* appears very attractive to Liberal Democratic Party politicians. Even among those who recognize the limited strategic value of an independent nuclear force, possession of nuclear weapons is seen as the key to membership in the world's most exclusive club, a way to dramatically demonstrate Japan's position as a great power and a means of gaining independence from the United States.

The "new nationalism," which has recently become the subject of much discussion in Japan, is largely expressed in terms of Japan playing a more "independent" and "positive" role in world affairs. The measure of independence is the degree to which Japanese policy differs from that of the United States. Japan has little to gain from a policy of greatly expanding its military force but stopping short of building nuclear weapons. It would consume national wealth that could be used for other purposes and would not provide the independence that would be the major selling point to the Japanese public. Present American policy looks to an increased Japanese military capability as a means of "burden sharing." In Japan, mounting popular support for such an increase does not result from a desire to share any burden with the United States but to gain greater autonomy in international politics. If Japan seeks to express its independence through its military might, the possession of nuclear weapons will be the inevitable consequence.

Some Americans look forward not only to a greater Japanese military defense capability but to Japan playing some kind of military role in East and Southeast Asia. This has not been expressed in official American policy but I think one might safely assume that the American Government would welcome a decision by Japan to send troops overseas to help insure "international peace and stability." The desire for a Japanese military role in Asia is based on questionable assumptions. For one thing there is no reason to believe that the Japanese military, if it could play an active role in Southeast Asia, would be any more successful than the United States has proven to be in Vietnam. Moreover, although the American military presence in Asia is resented because it looks too much like white domination over Asians, a much enlarged and active Japanese military would probably be feared as much if not more, and not only by states unfriendly to the United States but by such allies as South Korea. The prospects of the Japanese military protecting Asia against communist aggression is not a particularly comforting thought to Asians, whose memories of the Japanese military date back to the days of the Greater East Asia Co-Prosperity Sphere. Furthermore, a Japanese military active outside of Japan would be regarded as a threat by China and the Soviet Union and would escalate tensions rather than reduce them. Americans must also ponder the possibility that a more militarily powerful Japan would not necessarily undertake policies that would be in the interest of the United States.

A Japanese military role in Asia is inconceivable in the foreseeable future unless the nationalist trend in Japan is encouraged to seek expression in terms of military might. As I have tried to indicate, such a development in Japan's domestic political situation would not be in the interest of the United States. In the meantime American pressures for a greater military role, in the absence of a domestic consensus in Japan in support of such a role, can have seriously harmful consequences. At the minimum, the alliance will become increasingly strained as the Japanese Government resists American pressures and anti-Americanism increases among the public. Another possibility is that American pressures will create a level of domestic instability in Japan that will undermine the alliance. But probably the most likely consequence will be an attempt by the Japanese Government to combine anti-American nationalist sentiment *and* American demands behind an "independent" foreign policy that would involve an enormous expansion of the military and eventually the possession of nuclear weapons.

The challenge that faces American policy makers in the seventies is not to convince Japan to undertake policies similar to those that have caused enormous domestic and international problems for the United States. It is rather to decide what policies are most likely to deflect Japanese nationalism from being anti-American, strengthen the political base of the relationship and allow Japan to contribute most effectively to peace in Asia.

THE REVERSION OF OKINAWA

Reversion of Okinawa is prerequisite, so to speak, to a new era in Japanese-American relations. Although significant sectors of Japanese opinion demanded the unconditional return of Okinawa, the agreement to return the islands in 1972 according to the so-called "home island formula" (meaning United States bases there would be dealt with on the same terms as bases in the home islands) did satisfy majority opinion and accorded with the policy of the ruling Liberal Democratic Party. The agreement, reached during the Sato-Nixon talks of November 1969, came too late however. American failure to move more quickly to return the islands reinforced the arguments of those who condemn the United States as a neo-colonial power, provoked a tremendous degree of public indignation, and did much to direct Japanese nationalism into anti-American channels. Reversion now will do little to increase pro-American sentiment while reversion a few years ago would have done much in this regard.

Many strategic thinkers have argued convincingly that Okinawa is not necessary as a nuclear base, that indeed close-up bases have been rendered obsolete and even a liability in the age of the inter-continental ballistic missile. But military arguments, whether on the need for nuclear weapons in Okinawa or for the free use of the bases there, should not be the determining factors in American policy. Arguments of military necessity ignore the point that there are one million Japanese living in Japanese territory under the rule of the United States. By subordinating its political interests to the convenience of the military, the United States precipitated an unnecessary crisis in Japanese-American relations and made a mockery of its espoused defense of the principle of self-determination, a principle it has ostensibly sent half a million men to defend in Vietnam.[1]

[1] Some of the sections of the Joint Communique issued on November 24, 1969 by President Nixon and Prime Minister Sato dealing with Okinawa are as follows:

" 6. The Prime Minister emphasized his view that the time had come to respond to the strong desire of the people of Japan, of both the mainland and Okinawa, to have the administrative rights over Okinawa returned to Japan on the basis of the friendly relations between the United States and Japan and thereby to restore Okinawa to its normal status. The President expressed appreciation of the Prime Minister's view. The President and the Prime Minister also recognized the vital role played by United States forces in Okinawa in the present situation in the Far East. As a result of their discussion, it was agreed that the mutual security interests of the United States and Japan could be accommodated within arrangements for the return of the administrative rights over Okinawa to Japan. They therefore agreed that the two governments would immediately enter into consultations regarding specific arrangements for accomplishing the early reversion of Okinawa without detriment to the security of the Far East including Japan. They further agreed to expedite the consultations with a view to accomplishing the reversion during 1972 subject to the conclusion of these specific arrangements with the necessary legislative support. . .

" 7. The President and the Prime Minister agreed that, upon return of the administrative rights, the Treaty of Mutual Cooperation and Security and its related arrangements would apply to Okinawa without modification thereof. . .

" 8. The Prime Minister described in detail the particular sentiment of the Japanese people against nuclear weapons and the policy of the Japanese Government reflecting such sentiment. The President expressed his deep understanding and assured the Prime Minister that, without prejudice to the position of the United States Government with respect to the prior consultation system under the Treaty of Mutual Cooperation and Security, the reversion of Okinawa would be carried out in a manner consistent with the policy of the Japanese Government as described by the Prime Minister.

10. . . .The President and the Prime Minister decided to establish in Okinawa a Preparatory Commission in place of the existing Advisory Committee to the High Commissioner of the Ryukyu Islands for the purpose of consulting and coordinating locally on measures relating to preparation for the transfer of administrative rights, including necessary assistance to the Government of the Ryukyu Islands. . ."

Also the following section of paragraph 4: "The President and the Prime Minister expressed the strong hope that the war in Vietnam would be concluded before the return of the administrative rights over Okinawa to Japan. In

Continued on page 176

To make the seventies a new era in Japanese-American relations, the United States should move rapidly toward phasing out its bases in Japan, bases which have become a major source of tension in the relationship. The presence in the Pacific of the Seventh Fleet and technological developments in weapons systems have greatly reduced the need for the permanent stationing of troops in overseas forward bases. An arrangement by which the United States would have the right to port calls by the Seventh Fleet at Yokosuka and Sasebo, access to repair facilities, and the use in times of emergency of bases maintained by the Self Defense Forces would serve the needs of the American military and eliminate a major source of irritation in America's relations with Japan.

Public demands in the United States in the seventies for reductions in military expenditures make such a phasing out all the more desirable and feasible. In fact the United States has already made a move in this direction by announcing its intention to close down nearly fifty military installations in Japan and to move as quickly as possible to eliminate others. Interestingly, there was very little public reaction in Japan, favorable or unfavorable, to this decision. This is partly due to the fact that most of these installations were extremely small and of minor importance. But the major reason is that the reduction was interpreted as being primarily an economy measure and one that did not represent any basic change in American policy. In the absence of a clear and publicized decision to move toward the withdrawal of all permanently stationed personnel, there is little chance that the United States will gain much

Footnote 1 continued from page 175

this connection, they agreed that, should peace in Vietnam not have been realized by the time reversion of Okinawa is scheduled to take place, the two governments would fully consult with each other in the light of the situation at that time so that reversion would be accomplished without affecting the United States efforts to assure the South Vietnamese people the opportunity to determine their own political future without outside interference. The Prime Minister stated that Japan was exploring what role she could play in bringing about stability in the Indochina area."

political advantage from base reductions.

THE FUTURE OF THE SECURITY TREATY

The Security Treaty issue is the most difficult problem with which the United States and Japan must deal in the coming years. Unfortunately public discussion of the Security Treaty in the United States has been virtually nonexistent, while in Japan, as Professor Kamiya points out, the Treaty is often regarded as the source of all of Japan's problems. Much of the public opposition to the Treaty in Japan is the consequence of the presence of American bases. Accordingly the removal of these bases alone would go far in reducing the level of public dissatisfaction with the alliance. For one thing it would remove the "base problem," the affront to nationalist sensibilities that result from having foreign troops stationed on one's own soil, and the inevitable incidents of plane crashes, crimes and the like. It would also eliminate the major cause of the fear with which Japanese view the Treaty—that the presence of American bases could involve Japan in a war against its wishes.

However, opposition to the Treaty goes deeper than opposition to the presence of American bases. The present Security Treaty, though negotiated and ratified in 1960, is popularly regarded in Japan as the continuation of the original Treaty of 1952, which for many represented an extension of the Occupation. Since the end of the Pacific War there has never been a time when American troops have not been stationed on Japanese soil. Consequently, there are psychological factors that enter into Japanese opposition to "*anpo*," the Security Treaty, that could not be dealt with by mere readjustments within the present treaty structure.

The optimum solution, to my mind, would be the removal of all American troops from Japan and the negotiation of a new treaty of friendship that would indicate a clear American commitment to Japan's defense, eliminating

Article 6 of the present treaty which gives the United States the right to have bases in Japan for "the purpose of contributing to the security of Japan and the maintenance of international peace and security in the Far East." A commitment to come to Japan's aid in the case of direct aggression does not require the presence of American bases in Japan and there is no "free ride" involved in extending the American nuclear umbrella, particulary in light of the American desire that Japan sign the nuclear non-proliferation treaty.

It seems to me a mistake to continue to value Japan as a base from which to stage military operations in other parts of Asia and to insist that Japan make clear its position on whether the United States can use bases for combat operations in areas such as Korea in advance of the prior consultations provided for in the exchange of letters accompanying the 1960 Security Treaty.[2]

The military convenience of bases in Japan could not possibly offset the political costs of using them in certain situations. Furthermore, where there is a real commonality of interest, as I believe is the case with South Korea, insistence that Japan make a public pledge that it will allow the United States to use bases in Japan for combat operations reinforces the view that Japan has no real independence of action, that there is a strong element of distrust in the American attitude and that the prior consultation system, a major revision of the earlier Treaty arrangements, does not have much meaning.

The signing of a new treaty, however, will most likely be a problem for the decade of the eighties, not the seventies, and will necessitate a great educational effort in the United States to inform the public about our real interests in

---

[2]In the November 21 Sato-Nixon Joint Communique, Prime Minister Sato indicated that the security of Korea and the Taiwan Straits were of direct concern to the security of Japan. In a speech given on the same day as the issuance of the Communique the Prime Minister stated that in the case of an attack against South Korea, "the policy of the Government of Japan towards prior consultation would be to decide its position positively and promptly."

Japan and our obligations as a world power. If anything, anti-Security Treaty sentiment is likely to grow in the United States in the coming years, both among those on the left who want to show their solidarity with the anti-Treaty movement in Japan and others who want to return the United States to isolationism and among those on the right who will become increasingly disenchanted with a Japan that refuses to "share the burden." A revised treaty would probably have a more difficult time getting through the United States Senate than the Japanese Diet.

The question here, of course, is much larger than the question of American policy toward Japan. It is whether a reduction in American involvement in Asia in the seventies will be accompanied by any basic change in American foreign policy, or whether the United States will simply seek to have other countries such as Japan pick up a larger part of the "burden" previously carried by the United States. The thesis of this paper has been that the latter approach will be self defeating. Japan is not likely to be satisfied with such a role, and the reduction of tensions in Asia is not likely to be achieved by encouraging Japan to adopt such a posture.

Strains in the economic relationship, I would agree with Professor Jansen, will largely work themselves out. The magnitude of the trade is too enormous, and the interdependence of the economies too great, to allow for any major reversal in the continuing trend toward ever freer trade and investment. As Professor Kamiya remarks, the significance of expressed dissatisfaction with the economic relationship is the underlying source of discontent with the political relationship it symbolizes. It is probably the areas of intellectual, cultural and political exchange that need the most attention in the seventies. Despite intimate economic and political ties, there is still an enormous gulf in understanding between the people of the two countries.

THE NEED FOR DISENGAGEMENT

In the coming years the United States must relax the

180   *Gerald L. Curtis*

tight embrace in which it and Japan have been locked and forge a new relationship with a Japan that charts its own course in foreign affairs and seeks its own solutions to the problems of international peace. The post-war objective of insuring Japan's participation in America's alliance system and its cooperation with America's strategic policies cannot be successful in the context of revitalized Japanese nationalism and a multi-polar international political system. The long term interest of the United States will be better served by a Japan that is sometimes a critical friend than by a Japan that is an unstable or frustrated ally. American policy toward Japan in the seventies should be premised on the recognition that American interest will best be served by the existence of a peaceful, democratic and prosperous Japan that will contribute in its own way to reducing international tensions. The domestic political situations in Japan and the United States and the national interests of both countries demand that the "new era" of the seventies be an era of disengagement.

FINAL REPORT

of the

SECOND JAPANESE-AMERICAN ASSEMBLY

At the close of their discussions the participants in the Second Japanese-American Assembly reviewed the following report in plenary session. The report represents general agreement. However, no one was asked to sign it, and in view of the often differing opinions expressed during the course of the discussions, it must be clearly understood that not every participant agrees with every statement.

The relationship between the United States and Japan and their role in Asia have become the subject of serious public debate in both countries. While Japan and the United States share many common interests, there are significant differences in their views of the world and their respective roles in it. Furthermore, these views have not remained constant within each country but have been undergoing change.

There is today in the United States a great concern to solve pressing domestic problems such as poverty, race relations and a variety of urban ills. The American experience in Vietnam has generated a general questioning of America's foreign policy posture. American public opinion clearly desires a reduction in the overseas commitments of the United States, particularly in its military aspects. The timing and extent of this reduction are at issue but not the principle itself.

Japan's rapid industrial growth has created urgent pressures for attention to educational, urban, and environmental problems. At the same time its enormous economic power has contributed to an increase in national confidence. In this setting, America's desire to limit its commitments coincides with a changing political environment in Asia to create new choices and constraints for Japan. There is also a questioning of past policies and a public desire for a different, though still unspecified, role in international affairs.

Asia in the seventies will see a greater complexity in international relations than has heretofore existed in the postwar period. The Sino-Soviet split, the ongoing withdrawal of American troops from Vietnam, and internal developments in Asian countries are combining to create new challenges and new opportunities for the United States and Japan. Both countries must work out policies for the changing political environment in Asia appropriate to their respective capabilities and the desires of their publics.

Political instability will continue to characterize much of Asia in the 1970's, often as a result of the social and political strains of nation building. This will sometimes be constructive and not necessarily dangerous to world peace or subject to outside influence.

Japan will play a more influential role in Southeast Asia in the coming decade. This is partly the inevitable consequence of its position as the only highly advanced industrial nation in Asia. Japan thus has a unique opportunity further to participate and assist in the economic development of other Asian nations. This role, if fully accepted, would be extremely complex and challenging, given the great differences in stages of economic growth, political stability and other conditions among the states in the area. It will require greater involvement but should exclude any military role. By the same token, the United States too should seek new opportunities to increase its role in economic development programs. Both countries should place emphasis on multilateral means in this field.

It is highly desirable that both the United States and Japan try to normalize their relations with mainland China and to have it participate in a variety of international conferences and organizations. The continued isolation of China and the misunderstanding of intentions between China, Japan, and the United States pose obstacles to the reduction of tensions in Asia.

The existing tensions between China and the Soviet Union are not expected to decrease in the near future. On the contrary, an increase in the conflict is a possibility in the coming decade. Military conflict between China and the Soviet Union is not in the interests of either the United States or Japan.

The problem of Taiwan is a major concern of both the United States and Japan. Eventually it must be solved by the people of Taiwan and China themselves. There was vigorous discussion concerning this formulation, but differences of opinion could not be resolved.

The Vietnam War must be brought to a quick settlement. All efforts should be made to insure that the Vietnamese themselves be free to decide what type of regime they desire. Both the United States and Japan should aid the reconstruction and economic development of North and South Vietnam in the postwar period.

The form of reversion of Okinawa to Japan is the most urgent issue confronting the United States and Japan. The Okinawan problem is not only one of national sovereignty but also of the basic rights of the Okinawan people. It is imperative that a timetable for reversion be set within this year and that immediate steps be taken to provide for Okinawan participation in Japanese life during the process of transition. It was the general view that the return of the islands in such a manner as would place American bases there on the same terms as apply to bases in other parts of Japan is most desirable. However views favoring the immediate, unconditional return of Okinawa were also expressed. Okinawan reversion to Japan will remove a major irritant in United States-Japanese relations and will contribute to the development of great mutuality of interest between the two countries.

The problem of Korea is of direct concern to the United States and cannot be disregarded by Japan. We were in general agreed that forcible change of existing borders in the Korean peninsula would present serious problems to the United States and Japan, although we did not arrive at conclusions on the extent of this danger or counter measures to be taken.

Mutual security arrangements between the two countries must be considered in terms of the long range friendship between the United States and Japan. There was a wide variety of opinion ranging from abrogation to the indefinite continuation of the present Treaty without change. The prevailing view was that, in the immediate future, there was no alternative to automatic extension. However, dissatisfactions in both the United States and Japan clearly require that the Treaty be constantly examined and adjustments made as expeditiously as possible. Even under the present Treaty, the further reduction of American bases in Japan is desirable. It was generally agreed that both countries should work toward creating conditions under which the security of Japan and its neighbors could be insured without the presence of American bases.

Close relations between the United States and Japan are in part the result of their extensive economic ties. As great trading nations, both share a common interest in maximizing the opportunities for the freest possible world wide economic interaction. In this context it is imperative that both nations eliminate as quickly as possible barriers to trade and take necessary steps to insure the free movement of capital between the two countries. It was generally recognized that at this stage Japan should take the initiative in this regard in order to avert a vicious circle of retaliatory protectionist measures. The economies of both countries are sufficiently strong to make protectionist measures unnecessary.

There is unanimous agreement among Americans and Japanese that a friendly and equal relationship is of fundamental importance. As advanced industrial societies both countries share many common problems despite differences in language, culture, and historical experience. We both must improve our mass education systems, deal with the dissatisfactions of youth, make our cities more liveable, and make government and large organizations more responsive to the needs of society.

* * *

It was resolved in plenary session that the funds specified for cultural purposes in the repayment of Japan's debt to the United States be used for the creation of a foundation devoted to the fuller development of dialogue and the study of our common problems.

NOTES ON THE CONTRIBUTORS

GERALD L. CURTIS is Assistant Professor of Political Science at Columbia University. Professor Curtis was joint editor of *Japanese-American Relations II*, the final report of the second Shimoda Assembly.

FUJI KAMIYA is Professor of International Relations at Osaka Municipal University.

MARIUS B. JANSEN is Professor of Japanese History, Princeton University.

JAMES WILLIAM MORLEY is Professor of Political Science, Columbia University, and former director of the East Asian Institute.

SABURO OKITA is President of the Japanese Economic Research Center, Tokyo.

GEORGE McT. KAHIN is Director of the Southeast Asia Program at Cornell University.

MINEO NAKAJIMA is Lecturer in International Relations and Chinese Studies at the Tokyo University of Foreign Studies.

Index

Abegglen, James, 41
ABM, 5, 144
Advisory Commission to the High Commissioner of the Ryukyus, replaced, 175 (footnote)
Afghanistan, 100 (footnote), 143
Africa, Japanese imports from, 105
Afro-Asian Conference, 150
Agricultural White Paper 70 (footnote)
Aichi, Kiichi, Foreign Minister, 33, 96, 99
Alaska, Japanese investment in pulp plants, 95
Albania, 146
American Assembly, 44
Anglo-Japanese Alliance, 23
ANZAI Economic Mission, 11
ANZUS Security Pact, 130
ASEAN, 133 (footnote)
Asia and Pacific Council (ASPAC), 32
Asian Development Bank, Japanese participation in, 95, 96, 109, 112
Asian Security Organization, 6, 7
ASPAC, see Asia and Pacific Council
Australia, 105, 130

BADGE Automatic Warning Radar, 81
Ball, George, 38
Bonin Islands, 159, 165
Brazil, Japanese investment in, 95
Brezhnev, Leonid, 7
    Address of June 7, 1969, 128
    Suggests Asian Security Organization, 6, 143
Britain, see England

Brunei, 122 (footnote), 135
Bungei Shunju 26 (footnote)
Burma, 94, 100 (footnote), 109, 110, 119, 120, 121 (footnote), 127, 128 (footnote), 135, 136

Cambodia, 16, 94, 109, 118, 119, 121, 123, 128 (footnote), 146
CENTO, 142
Ceylon, 100 (footnote)
Chiang Kai-Shek, 159
China, 13, 21, 27, 28, 36, 45, 124
China
    Communist Party, 141, 148, 153
    containment of, 134, 144, 145
    Cultural Revolution, 7, 32, 34, 141, 144-149
    diplomatic threat, 151-152
    encouragement of subversion, 137-138
    GNP, 7, 39, 41
    "Great Leap Forward," 146
    ICBM, 144
    loss of, 115
    military intervention in Southeast Asia, 132, 135
    nuclear weapons, 5, 39, 145, 152-154
    relations with Japan, 21, 32, 39
    relations with Southeast Asia, 127-129
    relations with the U.S.S.R., 6, 7, 128-129, 141, 145-146
    relations with the United States, 39, 142, 145
    support of revolution, 150-151
    threat to the West, 149-154
China People's Daily 147

188   *Index*

Chou-En-Lai, comments on Chinese bomb, 152-153
Chongwadai Incident of Jan. 1968, 9
Committee for Economic Development, see *Keizai Doyukai*
Communism, international, 6, 115
Constitution and Education Rescript, 25
Cuba crisis of 1962, 140
Czechoslovakia, 6, 17, 141, 147, 159

Damansky Island incident, 6, 147
De Gaulle, Gen. Charles, 5, 140, 141
Development Assistance Committee, 112
Dulles, John Foster, 160, 161, 162, 163

EC-121 incident, 9, 10
E.C.A.F.E., 105
Economic Growth Center, Yale University, 49 (footnote)
Economic Planning Board, 49 (footnote)
Economic Warfare, 11
Economist, 152 (footnote)
Eisenhower, President Dwight D., Comments on Okinawa, 161
Communique with Kishi, 164
England, 5, 36, 41
Withdrawal East of Suez, 100, 142

F104Js, 81
F4E Phantoms, 33, 81
Five Principles of Peace, 151
Foreign Affairs, 38, 118 (footnote), 131
France, 5, 36, 41, 84, 140, 146
Fuji-Yawata, 41
Fukuda, Finance Minister, speech at Sidney, 96, 99
Fukuzawa, Yukichi, 25

"green revolution," 108
Great Britain, see England

"Greater East Asia Co-Prosperity Sphere," 173
Gromyko, Andrei, 7
"Guam Doctrine" of President Nixon, 142
Guinea, Chinese relations with, 146

Hanoi, 119
HAWK missile, 81
Hayashi, Fusao, 37
Hiroshima, 27
Hong Kong, 104, 105, 106, 107, 108, 150
Hungary, Nixon's gestures to, 12

ILO, 75 (footnote)
India, 27, 94, 100 (footnote), 106, 107, 136, 143
Indian Ocean, 7
Indo China, 118, 176 (footnote)
Indonesia, 16, 27, 36, 94, 106, 109, 110, 117, 120, 128 (footnote), 130, 133, 135, 150
Communist Party, 117
International Congress of Communist Parties, 143
International Labor Organization, 75 (footnote)
International Monetary Fund, 104
Inukai, Premier, murder of, 28
Ishihara, Shintaro, 27

Japan
agriculture, 67, 70, 71, 73, 92, 108, 109
Air Self-Defense Force, 81
Bureau of Statistics, 61 (footnote), 71 (footnote)
Communist Party, 1, 44
Constitution, 33, 34, 40, 157-158, 170
cooperatives, 70
Defense Agency, 162
Diet, 45, 90
domestic situation, 3
economic growth, 26, 48-49, 88
education, 75-77, 79, 81, 92
foreign aid, 84, 87-88, 107-110, 111-113
foreign investments, 94-96, 99

foreign trade, 18, 42, 62, 100, 101, 104-105, 106-107, 110-111
forestry, 67
"free ride," 12, 15, 162, 170, 178
GNP, 7, 11, 36, 39, 41, 43, 49, 52, 62, 65, 71, 73, 76, 79, 81, 82, 84, 87-88, 92, 96, 100, 110, 170
Imperial era, 25
labor, 52, 61, 70
Liberal-Democratic Party, 89, 90-91, 171, 174
Maritime Self-Defense Force, 81
military forces, 36, 81-82, 169-174
National Police Reserve, 162
Nationalism, 25, 26, 27, 37, 38, 45-46, 62, 172-174
northern islands, 32
nuclear weapons, 33, 36, 37, 46, 152, 171-172
Occupation, 157-158, 161, 163, 177-178
pacifism, 18, 19, 36
Peace Treaty, 159
population, 36, 65, 67
productivity, 36
rearmament, 161
relations with China, 21, 32, 39, 40, 155-156
relations with North Korea, 10
relations with South Korea, 10, 32
relations with Southeast Asia, 100-101, 104-105, 107-113, 129-130
relations with the U.S., 92, 155-185
relations with the U.S.S.R., 32
reparations, 94
research and development, 61-62, 65
"Rice Bank" concept, 101
Security Treaty, 1, 2, 3, 12, 15, 19, 23, 31, 45, 160, 161, 162, 163, 164, 175 (footnote), 177-180, 184

Self Defense Establishment, 28, 33, 45, 81, 162, 171, 176
social security in, 73, 75
Socialist Party, 4, 89
steel production, 41
student movements, 30, 31, 34, 44-45
trade with mainland China, 101
Treaty of Mutual Cooperation and Security, 164
"Unequal Treaties," 25
urbanization, 41-42, 65, 67, 71, 92
U.S. bases in, 12, 176
wages, 106, 107
youth, 89-90
Japan (Journal), 25
Japan and the Japanese (Journal), 25
Japan Economic Research Center, 49, 110
Japan Statistical Yearbook, 61 (footnote)
Jiyu, 39 (footnote)
Johnson, Lyndon Baines, 142, 149, 165
administration, 117, 131, 144
statement of March 31, 1968, 141

Kahn, Herman, 49 (footnote)
Kalimantan, 122
Kapsan Faction, 9
Kato, Hidetoshi, 22
Keizai Doyukai (Committee for Economic Development), 30, 44, 112
Kennedy, President John F., 140, 165
Kim Il-Song, 8, 9
Kishi, issues communique with Eisenhower, 164
Kissinger, Henry, 14
Kiuchi, represents Japan at 25th ECAFE General Assembly in Singapore, 96
Kodama, Yoshio, 30

Komeito, 45
Korea, 7, 183
  Five-Year Plan, 8
  Seven-Year Plan, 8, 9
  War, 162
  Workers Party Congress, 8
Kosygin, Premier, 143
Kruschev, Nikita, 8, 140, 152
Kuomintang Chinese Troops in Burma, 120

Laos, 94, 118, 119, 120, 121, 127, 128 (footnote), 130
Lattimore, Owen, 13
LDCs, 87
Liberation Army Bulletin, 147
Liberation Army Report, 153 (footnote)
Lin-Piao, 148, 150, 153-154
Liu Shao-Chi, 147, 149, 152

McNamara, Robert
  Secretary of Defense, 14
  McNamara Doctrine, 16

MacArthur, General Douglas, 25
  Establishes National Police Reserve, 162
Mainichi, Survey of July 1968, 30
Malaysia, 7, 41, 122, 123, 130, 133, 135
Manchuria, 28, 29
Mansfield, Senator, calls Nixon statement "the Guam Doctrine," 142
Mao Tse-Tung, 148, 150, 153, 159
  Thoughts, 146, 154
Maoists, 44
Masuda, (Security Agency Director General), 33
Meiji Restoration, 24, 25, 27
"Memorandum Trade," 32
Meo tribesmen, 120
Middle East, Japanese investment in oil, 95
Minas steel mill, Japanese investment in, 95
Ministry of Agriculture and Forestry, 70 (footnote)

Minseido, student organizations, 44
"miracle rice," 108
MIRV missile, 5
Monroe Doctrine, 16
Monthly Statistics of Japan, 71
Mutsu, Munemitsu, 23, 25
Mutual Security Pact, 82

Nasution, General, 117 (footnote)
National Liberation Front, 117
"New Czarism," 6
New Zealand, role in Southeast Asia, 130, 135
Nihon Kokusai zue, 75 (footnote)
NIKE-AJAX missiles, 81
Nixon, Richard, 12, 115, 144, 167, 175 (footnote), 178 (footnote)
  Article in *Foreign Affairs*, 118, 131
  Guam statement, 142
  President, 3, 10, 12, 14, 100, 115, 117
  Vice-President, 115, 161
  Vietnam policy, 142
North America, Japanese imports of raw materials, 105
North Korea, 8, 17, 27
North Vietnam, 27, 44, 119, 121 (footnote), 129, 134, 140, 146

O.E.C.D., Japanese membership in, 104
Ohama, Dr. Nobumoto, 26 (footnote)
Okinawa, 2, 26 (footnote), 82, 110, 159, 161
  reversion to Japan, 1, 12, 13, 14, 31, 35, 38, 44, 46, 82, 100, 164, 165, 170, 174-177, 183
  U.S. bases on, 31, 35, 167, 169
Okita, Saburo, 42
Overseas Chinese, 122-123, 133, 134

Pak Chong-hi, 8, 9, 10
Pakistan, 27, 106, 136, 143, 146
Passin, Herbert, 44
Patrick, Hugh, 49 (footnote)
Pearl Harbor, 27
Peking, 119

People's War, 147
PHANTOM airplanes, 33, 81
Philippines, 94, 110, 116, 117, 120,
    123, 126, 130, 133, 135, 136
The Phoenix Risen from the Ashes,
    49 (footnote)
Preparatory Commission on
    Okinawa, 175 (footnote)
"Pueblo" incident, 9

Red Flag, 147
Reischauer, Edwin, appointed
    Ambassador, 165
Rogers, William P, Secretary of
    State, 14
Rumania, 12, 146
Russia, see U.S.S.R.
Ryukyu Islands, 100 (footnote),
    175 (footnote)

Sabah, 122
Saeki, Kiichi, 39, 40, 41
"Safeguard" Project, 144
San Francisco Peace Treaty, 100
Sarawak, 121
Sasebo, 176
Sato, Prime Minister, 35, 149, 165,
    175 (footnote), 178 (footnote)
    Administration, 3, 91, 174
Schlesinger, Arthur, summarizes
    lessons of Vietnam war, 141-142
Science and Technology Agency, 62
    (footnote)
SEATO, 142
Security Pact (Japan-U.S.), see
    Japan, Security Treaty
"Sentinel" Program, 144
Shigemitsu, Prime Minister, 162
Shinjuku, violence, 27
Shishi, (political activists), 31
Shukan Gendai, 28 (footnote)
Siberia, Japanese imports from, 105
Singapore, 41, 106, 120, 130, 135
Sinkiang-Uigur Autonomous Region
    incidents, 6
Socialist Imperialism, 6, 147
Sohyo (labor federation), 89
Soka Gakkai, 45

South Korea, 8, 9, 16, 17, 27, 40,
    41, 42, 104, 105, 106, 107, 108,
    110, 120, 173, 178
    Exports, 18
    Five Year Plan, 9, 94, 95
South Vietnam, 14, 27, 115, 119,
    121
Southeast Asia
    borders, 121
    change in, 120-127
    insurgency, 132, 138-139
    neutralization of, 136-137
    subversion, 138-139
    U.S. policy in, 114-139
Southeast Asian Ministerial
    Conference for Economic
    Development, 96, 109
Soviet Union, see U.S.S.R.
Space Activities Council, 36
Stalin, 8
Suharto, General, 117
Supreme Soviet, 7
Sweden, amount spent on Social
    Security, 75

Taiwan, 40, 41, 42, 45, 95, 104,
    105, 106, 107, 108, 120, 133,
    144, 178 (footnote), 183
Tanzania, Chinese relations with,
    146
Thailand, 41, 106, 109, 110, 117,
    118, 119, 120, 121, 126, 127,
    127 (footnote), 133 (footnote),
    135, 136, 167
Third Defense Build-up Program, 81
Tokaido, 43
Tokugawa Feudalism, 25
Trotskyites, 44
Truman, President Harry S., 141

U.S.S.R., 13, 28, 124, 151, 159
    relations with China, 6, 7,
        128-129, 140, 142, 154-156
    relations with Japan, 40
    relations with Korea, 10
    relations with Southeast Asia,
        128, 128 (footnote), 129,
        142, 143

192   *Index*

relations with the United States,
5, 134, 136, 140, 144
United Kingdom, see England
United Nations, 45, 144, 145
United States, 84
Dept. of Defense, 14, 161
domestic situation, 3
GNP, 11, 52, 62
isolationism, 168-169
relations with China, 22-23, 144,
145-146
relations with Japan, 157-185
relations with South Korea, 10
relations with Southeast Asia,
114-139
relations with the U.S.S.R., 5,
134, 136, 140, 144
Seventh Fleet, 176
Special Forces, 119
United States and Japan, 44, 100
United States-Japan Businessmen's
Conference, 11
United States-Japan Security Treaty,
see Japan, Security Treaty
U.S.-Philippines Security Pact, 130
U.S. Steel Co., 41
University Law, 3

Vietnam, 108, 117, 118, 119, 127,
127 (footnote), 130, 131, 135,
140, 142, 145
effect of Japan-U.S. relations,
166-168

war in, 1, 2, 3, 5, 11, 12, 14,
17, 100, 107, 114-120, 132,
146, 175 (footnote), 183
Workers Party, 150

Wakaizumi, Professor, 40
Wallace, George, 115
Weimar Germany, 27
Weiner, Anthony J., 49 (footnote)
West Germany, foreign aid, 84
West Irian, 121
*White Paper on Science and
Technology*, 62 (footnote)
World Bank, 112
World Communist Party Congress,
5-6, 7
World War II, 15
Wright, Frank Lloyd, 24

Yale University, 49 (footnote)
Yano Tsuneta kinenkai, 75
(footnote)
Yao tribesmen, 120
The Year 2000, 49 (footnote)
YMCA, regarded as subversive by
Imperial China, 138
Yokosuka, 176
Yomiuri Survey, 1969, 19
Yoshida, 35
Yugoslavia, 36, 146

Zambia, Chinese relations with, 146
Zengakuren, 45

THE JAPAN COUNCIL

FOR

INTERNATIONAL UNDERSTANDING

(Akasaka Tokyu Building, Tokyo)

The Japan Council for International Understanding was founded in 1962 by Japanese business and civic leaders. Its purpose is to stimulate research and discussion on international issues.

The Japan Council endeavors through regular contacts with foreign organizations of a similar nature to maintain a flow of information between Japan and other free nations on an unofficial basis.

Through the efforts of the Japan Council, Japanese leaders from many fields of specialization are afforded an opportunity to candidly exchange views with leaders of other countries in informal settings.

PARTICIPANTS

IN THE

SECOND JAPANESE-AMERICAN ASSEMBLY

Joint Chairmen

Tokusaburo Kosaka
Chairman
Japan Council for International
  Understanding
Tokyo

Clifford C. Nelson
President
The American Assembly
Columbia University
New York

Joint Editors

Gerald L. Curtis
Assistant Professor of Political
  Science
Columbia University

Fuji Kamiya
Professor of International Relations
Osaka Municipal University

Chief Administrator

and

Liaison Officer

Tadashi Yamamoto
Japan Council for International
Understanding

SHIGEYOSHI AIKAWA
Adviser to Editorial Board
Yomiuri Shinbun

YOSHIKATA ASO
Member, House of Representatives
Democratic Socialist Party

HANS H. BAERWALD
Visiting Professor
International Christian University
Tokyo

A. DOAK BARNETT
Brookings Institution
Washington, D.C.

JOHN BRADEMAS
Representative from Indiana
Congress of the United States

WILLIAM E. BROCK
Representative from Tennessee
Congress of the United States

JEROME COHEN
Professor of Law
Harvard University

FREDERICK DUTTON
Executive Director
The Robert F. Kennedy
  Memorial Foundation

JOHN EMMERSON
Professor of Political Science
Stanford University

JUN ETO
Literary Critic and Author

THOMAS S. FOLEY
Representative from Washington
Congress of the United States

AIICHIRO FUJIYAMA
Member, House of Representatives
Liberal Democratic Party

MOTOO GOTO
Assistant Editorial Writer
The Asahi Shinbun

NOBORU GOTO
President
Tokyo Electric Railway, Ltd.

KAZUSHIGE HIRASAWA
Editor-in-Chief
The Japan Times

STANLEY HOFFMAN
Professor of Government
Harvard University

HIROKI IMAZATO
President
Nippon Seiko K. K.

ROKURO ISHIKAWA
Vice-President
Kajima Construction Co., Ltd.

MARIUS B. JANSEN
Professor of Japanese History
Princeton University

NICHOLAS JOHNSON
United States Federal
   Communications Commissioner

MOTOO KAEDE
Sub-Chief Editor
Tokyo Chunichi Shinbun

GEORGE McT. KAHIN
Director
Southeast Asia Program
Cornell University

RAYMOND A. KATHE
Senior Vice President
First National City Bank

SHOJIRO KAWASHIMA
Member, House of Representatives
Vice-Chairman of the Party
Liberal Democratic Party

YOHEI KOHNO
Member, House of Representatives
Liberal Democratic Party

ZENTARO KOSAKA
Member, House of Representatives
Liberal Democratic Party
Former Foreign Affairs Minister

MASATAKA KOHSAKA
Professor of Law
Kyoto University

HIROSHI KUROKAWA
Assistant Managing Editor
Nihon Keizai Shinbun

AKIRA KUROYANAGI
Member, House of Councilors
Vice Secretary, Komeito

SHIGEHARU MATSUMOTO
Chairman
Board of Directors
International House of Japan, Inc.

SHIRO MIKUMO
Chief Editorial Writer
The Sankei Shinbun

SEIGEN MIYAZATO
Professor of Law
Ryukyu University
Okinawa

OSAMU MIYOSHI
Editorial Writer
The Mainichi Newspapers

JAMES W. MORLEY
Professor of Political Science
Columbia University

KINHIDE MUSHAKOJI
President
Institute of International Relations
   for Advanced Study of Peace
   and Development in Asia

EIICHI NAGASUE
Member, House of Representatives
Member, Central Executive Committee
Democratic Socialist Party

MINEO NAKAJIMA
Lecturer in International Relations
   and Chinese Studies
Tokyo University of Foreign Studies

YASUHIRO NAKASONE
Member, House of Representatives
Liberal Democratic Party

YASUMASA OHTA
Sub-Chief Editorial Writer
The Kyodo Press

HERBERT PASSIN
Professor of Sociology
Columbia University

HUGH PATRICK
Professor of Far Eastern Economics
Yale University

CHARLES PERCY
United States Senator
   from Illinois

RICHARD PFEFFER
Assistant Professor
Dept. of Political Science
Johns Hopkins University

GERALD PIEL
President and Publisher
Scientific American

JOHN POWERS
Aspen Institute
Colorado

EDWIN O. REISCHAUER
Professor
Department of Asian Studies
Harvard University

DONALD RUMSFELD
Director
Office of Economic Opportunity
Washington, D.C.

KIICHI SAEKI
President
Nomura Research Institute of
   Technology and Economics

SHOICHI SAEKI
Professor of Literature
Tokyo University

JIRO SAKAMOTO
Professor
Hitotsubashi University

JOSEPH E. SLATER
President
The Salk Institute

WILLIAM A. STEIGER
Representative from Wisconsin
Congress of the United States

NATHANIEL B. THAYER
New York

S. FLETCHER THOMPSON, JR.
Representative from Georgia
Congress of the United States

SEIJI TSUTSUMI
President
Seibu Department Store Co., Ltd.

JOHN V. TUNNEY
Representative from California
Congress of the United States

GORDON TWEEDY
Chairman
C. V. Starr & Co., Ltd.
New York

MORRIS UDALL
Representative from Arizona
Congress of the United States

KOGORO UEMURA
President
Japan Federation of Economic
    Organizations

JIRO USHIO
President
Ushio Electric Co., Ltd.

ARTHUR L. WADSWORTH
Executive Vice-President
Dillon Read & Co.
New York

KEI WAKAIZUMI
Professor of International Relations
Kyoto Sangyo University

ICHIRO WATANABE
Member, House of Representatives
Komeito

ROBERT M. WHITE II
Editor & Publisher
The Mexico Ledger
Missouri

MASAKAZU YAMAZAKI
Playwright
Assistant Professor
Kansai University

THE AMERICAN ASSEMBLY

The American Assembly was established by Dwight D. Eisenhower at Columbia University in 1950. It holds nonpartisan meetings and publishes authoritative books to illuminate issues of United States policy.

An affiliate of Columbia, with offices in the Graduate School of Business, the Assembly is a national, educational institution incorporated in the State of New York.

The Assembly seeks to provide information, stimulate discussion, and evoke independent conclusions in matters of vital public interest.

AMERICAN ASSEMBLY SESSIONS

At least two national programs are initiated each year. Authorities are retained to write background papers presenting essential data and defining the main issues in each subject.

About 60 men and women representing a broad range of experience, competence, and American leadership meet for several days to discuss the Assembly topic and consider alternatives for national policy.

All Assemblies follow the same procedure. The background papers are sent to participants in advance of the Assembly. The Assembly meets in small groups for four or five lengthy periods. All groups use the same agenda. At the close of these informal sessions participants adopt in plenary session a final report of findings and recommendations.

Regional, state, and local Assemblies are held following the national session at Arden House. Assemblies have also been held in England, Switzerland, Malaysia, Canada, the Caribbean, South America, Central America, Japan and the Philippines. Over one hundred institutions have co-sponsored one or more Assemblies.

AMERICAN ASSEMBLY BOOKS

The background papers for each Assembly program are published in cloth and paperbound editions for use by individuals, libraries, businesses, public agencies, nongovernmental organizations, educational institutions, discussion and service groups. In this way the deliberations of Assembly sessions are continued and extended.

American Assembly books are purchased and put to use by thousands of individuals, libraries, business, public agencies, nongovernmental organizations, educational institutions, discussion meetings and service groups. Since 1960 Assembly books have been published by Prentice-Hall, Inc., Frederick A. Praeger, Inc., and Columbia Books, Inc. The subjects of Assembly studies to date are:

1951–UNITED STATES-WESTERN EUROPE
      RELATIONSHIPS
1952–INFLATION
1953–ECONOMIC SECURITY FOR AMERICANS
1954–THE UNITED STATES STAKE IN THE UNITED
      NATIONS
     –THE FEDERAL GOVERNMENT SERVICE
1955–UNITED STATES AGRICULTURE
     –THE FORTY-EIGHT STATES
1956–THE REPRESENTATION OF THE UNITED
      STATES ABROAD
     –THE UNITED STATES AND THE FAR EAST
1957–INTERNATIONAL STABILITY AND PROGRESS
     –ATOMS FOR POWER
1958–THE UNITED STATES AND AFRICA
     –UNITED STATES MONETARY POLICY
1959–WAGES, PRICES, PROFITS AND PRODUCTIVITY
     –THE UNITED STATES AND LATIN AMERICA
1960–THE FEDERAL GOVERNMENT AND HIGHER
      EDUCATION
     –THE SECRETARY OF STATE
     –GOALS FOR AMERICANS

1961–ARMS CONTROL: ISSUES FOR THE PUBLIC
 –OUTER SPACE: PROSPECTS FOR MAN AND
   SOCIETY
1962–AUTOMATION AND TECHNOLOGICAL
   CHANGES
 –CULTURAL AFFAIRS AND FOREIGN
   RELATIONS
1963–THE POPULATION DILEMMA
 –THE UNITED STATES AND THE MIDDLE EAST
1964–THE UNITED STATES AND CANADA
 –THE CONGRESS AND AMERICA'S FUTURE
1965–THE COURTS, THE PUBLIC AND THE LAW
   EXPLOSION
 –THE UNITED STATES AND JAPAN
1966–THE UNITED STATES AND THE PHILIPPINES
 –STATE LEGISLATURES IN AMERICAN POLITICS
 –A WORLD OF NUCLEAR POWERS?
 –POPULATION DILEMMA IN LATIN AMERICA
 –CHALLENGES TO COLLECTIVE BARGAINING
1967–THE UNITED STATES AND EASTERN EUROPE
 –OMBUDSMEN FOR AMERICAN GOVERNMENT?
1968–LAW IN A CHANGING AMERICA
 –THE USES OF THE SEAS
 –WORLD HUNGER
1969–THE POPULATION DILEMMA
1969–BLACK ECONOMIC DEVELOPMENT
 –THE STATES AND THE URBAN CRISIS
1970–THE HEALTH OF AMERICANS
 –JAPANESE-AMERICAN RELATIONS IN THE
   1970s

Second Editions:

1962–THE UNITED STATES AND THE FAR EAST
1963–THE UNITED STATES AND LATIN AMERICA
 –THE UNITED STATES AND AFRICA
1964–UNITED STATES MONETARY POLICY

1965—THE FEDERAL GOVERNMENT SERVICE
  —THE REPRESENTATION OF THE UNITED
    STATES ABROAD
1968—OUTER SPACE: PROSPECTS FOR MAN AND
    SOCIETY
  —CULTURAL AFFAIRS AND FOREIGN
    RELATIONS

The American Assembly

Columbia University

φ6176φ2φ

JAPANESE-AMERICAN
RELATIONS
IN THE 1970s

Edited by Professor Gerald L. Curtis, Columbia University

The Second Japanese-American Assembly, sponsored by the Japan Council for International Understanding and The American Assembly, met in Shimoda, Japan, September 4-7, 1969. As in the first Assembly, also held in Shimoda, in 1967, the 70 participants included scholars, government officials, businessmen and communications specialists from both nations.

For three days in small groups they discussed the outlook for relations between the United States and Japan during the next decade in view of the rapidly evolving political, economic and social situations in these two countries and the rest of the world.

The papers presented at the Assembly are gathered in this volume, together with a summary and the conclusions of the Editor.

Japan today is the third most productive country in the world, and the most important ally of the United States in Asia. Our future policy toward this crowded land of 100,000,000 highly gifted and energetic people will have significant effect on the life of every American.

The facts, background and conclusions reported here are "must" reading for anyone interested in our future policies in Asia and the Western Pacific.

Columbia Books, Inc., Publishers
917 15th Street, N.W.